W9-BLL-585

# Is Jesus the Only Savior?

## Other Books by Ronald H. Nash

*Great Divides: Understanding the Controversies that Come Between Christians*

*Beyond Liberation Theology*

*Worldviews in Conflict*

*Poverty and Wealth: Why Socialism Doesn't Work*

*The Word of God and the Mind of Man*

*The Gospel and the Greeks: Did the New Testament Borrow From Pagan Thought?*

*The Closing of the American Heart: What's Really Wrong With America's Schools?*

*Choosing a College*

*Faith and Reason: Searching for a Rational Faith*

*Social Justice and the Christian Church*

*Liberation Theology (editor)*

*Christian Faith and Historical Understanding*

*The Concept of God*

*Freedom, Justice and the State*

*The Light of the Mind: St. Augustine's Theory of Knowledge*

# Is JESUS the Only SAVIOR?

## RONALD H. NASH

ZondervanPublishingHouse
*Grand Rapids, Michigan*

*A Division of* HarperCollins*Publishers*

Queries may be addressed to:
    Zondervan Publishing House
    5300 Patterson Avenue S.E.
    Grand Rapids, Michigan 49530.

*Library of Congress Cataloging-in-Publication Data*
Nash, Ronald H.
        Is Jesus the only savior? / Ronald H. Nash
            p. cm.
        Includes bibliographical references and index.
        ISBN 0-310-44391-1 (pbk.)
        1. Salvation outside the church. 2. Jesus Christ — History of doctrines — 20th century. 3. Religious pluralism. 4. Hick, John. I. Title.
BT759.N37     1994

                                                            94-8317

261.2 — dc20

                                                                    CIP

*Printed in the United States of America*

 94 95 96 97 98 99 /❖ ML/ 10 9 8 7 6 5 4 3 2 1

*To Andrew Michael Nash*

# CONTENTS

# PREFACE

Once upon a time Christians were identifiable by an unqualified commitment to Jesus Christ as the one and only Savior of the world. But the unity of Christians on this fundamental issue has disappeared. Today many people who claim to be Christians choose among three fundamentally different answers to the question, "Is Jesus the only Savior?" These answers can be stated succinctly:

No!

Yes, but . . .

Yes, period!

The negative answer — the belief that Jesus is not the only Savior — is commonly called *pluralism*. People holding this view think that there are many paths to salvation and that Jesus is only one of them.

The unqualified affirmative answer (Yes, period!) is undoubtedly the one that most readers of this book identify with. This view is often called *exclusivism* because it teaches that there is one exclusive way whereby men and women can approach God and receive his salvation: Jesus Christ. Sometimes this position is called *restrictivism* because it teaches that salvation is restricted to people who come to have explicit faith in Jesus Christ.

The qualified affirmative answer (Yes, but . . . ) is the favored view of a growing number of Christian college and seminary professors. But it is also held by many pastors, Christian workers, and denominational leaders who were introduced to the theory by their professors. This position is commonly called *inclusivism* because its adherents believe that the scope of God's salvation is significantly wider than that held by exclusivists. It is so wide or broad that it includes many people who have not explicitly believed in Jesus.

This book examines these three competing views, identifies some of their major proponents, and explains why they believe as they do, with a view to determining which is true.

Why should the reader care about these issues? For one thing, pluralism and inclusivism dramatically alter the nature of the Christian faith. Pluralism is one of the three or four most serious threats to the integrity of the Christian faith at the end of the twentieth century.[1] When people adopt pluralism, they *must* abandon every core doctrine of the Christian faith, including the Trinity, the deity of Christ, the Incarnation, and the Atonement. Inclusivism has a significant deleterious effect on the nature and importance of such Christian activities as evangelism and missions.

My book is hardly the first on this subject, as the bibliography shows, but right now it is the only book I know of that defends the exclusivist position in the context of the current debate. This book also differs from others by what I trust is its greater accessibility to the nonspecialized reader. Where the material gets difficult, I have tried to simplify as much as possible without doing an injustice to my sources. The reader will encounter a minimal number of technical terms and complex ideas. But I believe I have managed to explain the terms and ideas in a way that even novices will find understandable.

I want to acknowledge the help and assistance of a number of people. Dr. Doug Geivett of Talbot Theological Seminary and Dr. Ken Gentry, Jr., of Christ College (Greenville, S.C.) read the entire manuscript and offered many helpful suggestions. I also appreciate the help provided by Paul Eddy, Brad Stetson, and David Melvin of the National Association of Evangelicals; Dr. Roger Nicole, my colleague at Reformed Theological Seminary – Orlando; and Amy Sherman, editor of *Stewardship Journal*.

---

1. I have examined these other challenges in various books. For discussions of liberation theology, see Humberto Belli and Ronald Nash, *Beyond Liberation Theology* (Grand Rapids: Baker, 1992), as well as my *Poverty and Wealth* (Dallas: Probe Books, 1992) and *Liberation Theology* (Grand Rapids: Baker, 1988). For treatments of process theology, see Ronald Nash, ed., *Process Theology* (Grand Rapids: Baker, 1987) and my book *The Concept of God* (Grand Rapids: Zondervan, 1983). For an introduction to feminist theology, see my *Great Divides* (Colorado Springs: NavPress, 1993).

Chapter One

# IS JESUS THE ONLY SAVIOR?

Three conflicting answers to the question "Is Jesus the only Savior?" spark a debate that is dividing religious thinkers in the English-speaking world. This chapter explains the oldest of the three views, Christian exclusivism, the position that answers our question with an unqualified yes. The other two answers, pluralism and inclusivism, arise mainly out of opposition to exclusivism.

I have three major reasons for writing this book: (1) To see whether pluralism succeeds in developing a strong enough case against exclusivism to lead thoughtful people to abandon the Christian church's historic teaching that Jesus is the only Savior (part 1); (2) to see whether inclusivism succeeds in developing a strong enough case against exclusivism to lead thoughtful Christians to embrace inclusivism (part 2); and (3) to present at least some of the reasons why many thoughtful and conscientious Christians continue to espouse Christian exclusivism.

## A DEFINITION OF CHRISTIAN EXCLUSIVISM

Christian exclusivism can be defined as the belief that (1) Jesus Christ is the *only* Savior, and (2) explicit faith in Jesus Christ is necessary for salvation. The first claim denies that there are or can be other saviors, a fact that distinguishes it from pluralism. The second claim denies that people may be saved without conscious and explicit faith in Jesus Christ, which sets it apart from inclusivism. Christian exclusivists begin by believing that the tenets of one religion — in this case, Christianity — are true and that any religious beliefs that are logically incompatible with those tenets are false.

## EXCLUSIVISM AND BIBLICAL AUTHORITY

Some people cannot understand why the Bible plays such a normative role in Christian thinking. Such people need to recognize that while humans are free to reject the authority of Scripture, they will only substitute some other authority in its place. Usually that authority is either their own opinions or those of other people. Christians believe that the Bible is God's special revelation "inscripturated," or communicated in writing. People who think this way understandably prefer the authority of God to that of some fallen and fallible human being.

The church's access to truth cannot be credited to the natural, human wisdom of its apostles. Rather, it lies in the fact that God himself has graciously revealed himself and truth about himself to select individuals who have given the church an inscripturation of that revealed truth in the Bible.

Many who teach in self-described Christian seminaries and colleges today do not believe and probably do not understand this time-honored notion of revealed truth.

To a great extent, much nonorthodox theology over the past two hundred years is a chronicle of futile attempts to retain respectability for religious faith while denying Christianity access to revealed truth. About the only thing such thinkers can agree on is that God has not spoken and, indeed, cannot speak. And even if God could speak, according to this view, humans are incapable of understanding whatever he might say. The human relationship to God, therefore, must be understood according to some model other than that of receiving information or truth. Instead, it must be understood as an inward personal experience with God devoid of any objective, cognitive means of testing its validity.

Influenced by such views, many theologians and clergy trivialize or repudiate the central role that revealed truth has played in the Christian religion. Knowledge about God is simply declared impossible and replaced by personal encounter, religious feeling, trust, or obedience. This relatively new teaching clashes with the traditional view that divine special revelation is a communication of truth and that human knowledge of this revealed truth is essential to any personal relationship with God.

A study of the literature reveals that religious thinkers who reject the possibility of revealed truth seldom bother to support their position with arguments.[1] Their theory has simply become part of the theological mind-set in many departments of religion. Moreover, the doctrine of revealed truth that is so widely rejected today is a straw man — a false target. And finally, the most serious problems with their noncognitive (noninformational) view of revelation are simply ignored.[2] The theological agnosticism that is such an important feature of contemporary nonorthodox theology marks a dramatic break with a major tradition of historic Christianity, a tradition that has affirmed both an intelligible revelation from God and a divinely given human ability to know the transcendent God through the medium of true propositions.

English philosopher John Hick is the major representative of pluralism. We will study his views in great detail in chapters 2 – 6. John Hick professes to have experienced an evangelical kind of Christian conversion when he was nineteen years old and also reports that his early Christian beliefs were generally conservative or orthodox.[3] How did Hick come gradually to renounce every essential Christian belief he once affirmed? The obvious starting point lies in his defective understanding of divine revelation and Scripture. Hick's capitulation to the prevailing neo-liberal or neo-orthodox view of Scripture was apparent

---

1. For an extended defense of major points made in this section, see Ronald Nash, *The Word of God and the Mind of Man* (Phillipsburg, N.J.: Presbyterian and Reformed, 1992). Regarding my last sentence, see chapters 1 – 4.

2. See chapters 3 and 4 of *The Word of God and the Mind of Man.*

3. For more detail on Hick's development from early "evangelical" to later pluralist, see Paul R. Eddy, "John Hick's Theological Pilgrimage," *Proceedings of the Wheaton College Theology Conference* (1993), vol. 1, *The Challenge of Religious Pluralism: An Evangelical Analysis and Response,* 26 – 38.

by the time he published his book *Faith and Knowledge* in 1957.[4]
Paul Eddy explains:

> Although [Hick] had definitely departed from evangelical
> theology with his adoption of a non-propositional view of
> revelation and the attendant implications for the Scriptures,
> he nonetheless maintained a generally conservative, if neo-
> orthodox theology. The problem, of course, was that the
> philosophical foundations for such a theology had been se-
> verely undercut by his religious epistemology. In tracing
> Hick's theological pilgrimage from this point on, one is pri-
> marily tracing the effects of the logical implications of his reli-
> gious philosophy [that is, his defective understanding of
> special revelation] upon this theology. Thus, one could argue
> that nearly every major theological development throughout
> the next four decades was in one sense or another implicit in
> this early religious philosophy.[5]

While Eddy applauds Hick's early commitment to such essential Christian beliefs as the Incarnation, he points out that the
basis for Hick's actions was less than stable:

> In faithfulness to his views of non-propositional revelation
> and the epistemological primacy of religious experience, Hick
> finds the cognitive grounds for Christological orthodoxy not
> in a cognitively-based revelation of truth from God, but
> rather in the very human attempts of the early Christian com-
> munity to formulate what they perceived to be the theologi-
> cal implications of their religious experience of Jesus. With
> this as a model, it is not surprising to find Hick's entire theol-
> ogy continuously spiraling away from its original orthodox
> source.[6]

In other words, Hick retained a generally orthodox theology
at the same time he had abandoned the epistemological foundation for those beliefs. Something had to give, and eventually it

---

4. John Hick, *Faith and Knowledge* (Ithaca, N.Y.: Cornell University Press, 1957). In chapter 2 of *The Word of God and the Mind of Man,* I point out how much modern theological agnosticism traces back to the work of the German philosopher Immanuel Kant (1724–1804). Eddy discusses the influence of Kant's philosophy upon Hick's evolving agnosticism in "John Hick's Theological Pilgrimage," 28.

5. Eddy, "John Hick's Theological Pilgrimage," 29.

6. Ibid., 30.

did. One by one, the early orthodox beliefs of John Hick disappeared from his system of thought. And as with almost all his
neo-liberal peers, it apparently never occurred to Hick to examine critically the faulty presuppositions that had led him to deny
even the possibility of divinely revealed truth.

My own critical examination of those unsupported, neo-liberal assumptions is the subject of an earlier book.[7] When theologians begin to think that knowledge about God is impossible
and that religious truth is unimportant, it is only a matter of
time until doctrines and creeds lose their relevance. Why worry
about denials of Christian creeds if doctrine and truth are unimportant? Hick started down that path, and we will see where he
ended up. Regrettably, many self-described evangelical thinkers
today find Hick's starting point acceptable. In this book we will
see how *their* faulty understanding of divine revelation may
have contributed to their own theological wanderings.

In another book I explained that every human being approaches life and thought from the perspective of some worldview, a comprehensive system of beliefs offering answers to
life's ultimate questions.[8] I also showed that many people do not
realize that they even have a worldview. For that reason, many
are also unaware of the content of their worldview and how it
controls the way they think and live.

The Christian worldview is related to the Bible in at least
two important ways. First, the basic assumption of the Christian
worldview is the belief that *human beings and the universe in
which they reside are the creation of the God who has revealed himself
in Scripture.* This link between God and the Scriptures is both
proper and necessary. It would be foolish for Christians to drive
a wedge between God and his self-disclosure in the canon of
Scripture. We have already seen what this did to John Hick's
thinking.

Second, the content of the Christian worldview is derived
from God's special revelation in the Bible. What this basically
means is that if the Christian worldview passes the tests that
should be applied to every worldview, this success reflects back

7. See Nash, *The Word of God and the Mind of Man.*
8. See Ronald Nash, *Faith and Reason* (Grand Rapids: Zondervan, 1988), chaps.
2 – 4.

positively upon the basic control-belief of the Christian's worldview (expressed in the previous paragraph). Any positive appraisal of that belief must then reflect favorably upon the Christian's basic religious authority, the Bible.[9] Since the biblical worldview passes the appropriate tests, the religious authority from which that worldview is drawn receives support from the same procedure. In other words, the Bible does not somehow get plugged into the process through some kind of irrational, blind "leap of faith."

All of this means that Christians have a right to draw their convictions from Scripture and to test the claims of other Christians against the teaching of the Bible. They would be both foolish and inconsistent to do otherwise.

## EXCLUSIVISM AND THE NEW TESTAMENT

Christian exclusivists believe that the New Testament affirms their position in several different but complementary ways. First, the New Testament repeatedly declares that salvation comes only through faith in Jesus Christ. One of many passages with this message is John 3:16 – 18:

> For God so loved the world that he gave his one and only Son, that whoever believes in him shall not perish but have eternal life. For God did not send his Son into the world to condemn the world, but to save the world through him. Whoever believes in him is not condemned, but whoever does not believe stands condemned already because he has not believed in the name of God's one and only Son.

In these words Jesus himself not only states that those who believe in him have eternal life but also warns that those who do not believe stand condemned.

In another familiar text, Jesus asserts in no uncertain terms, "I am the way and the truth and the life. No one comes to the Father except through me" (John 14:6).

---

9. See Ronald Nash, *Worldviews in Conflict* (Grand Rapids: Zondervan, 1992), chaps. 1 – 5.

Of course, both these passages appear in the gospel of John and, as we will see, pluralists do not like the fourth gospel. Because it contains so much material that conflicts with their position, pluralists dismiss the authenticity of this gospel and the words it attributes to Jesus. Jesus, they contend, could never or would never have uttered the many "offensive" statements that appear in the fourth gospel.[10] No one who believes such statements could possibly be a pluralist. I will evaluate this dismissal of biblical material later, but for now we must see how exclusivism is clearly taught elsewhere in the New Testament.

Exclusivism is obviously taught in the book of Acts, which is Luke's extension of his gospel. In Acts 4:12, Peter proclaims that "Salvation is found in no one else, for there is no other name under heaven given to men by which we must be saved." Acts 8 relates that the Ethiopian eunuch is saved when Philip builds on his interest in Isaiah 53 and connects that passage to the good news about Jesus (Acts 8:35). When the Philippian jailer asks Paul and Silas what he must do to be saved, they reply, "Believe in the Lord Jesus, and you will be saved" (Acts 16:31).

Paul's epistle to the Romans is a detailed analysis of the nature and ground of justification, the act by which God imputes Christ's righteousness to sinful humans who have trusted in Jesus. Paul makes it clear that the one and only ground of human justification before the holy God is the atoning work of Jesus Christ (see Romans 3:10 – 28; 5:1 – 11). In Romans 10, Paul explains how sinful men attain the righteousness that saves: "That if you confess with your mouth, 'Jesus is Lord,' and believe in your heart that God raised [Jesus] from the dead, you will be saved" (v. 9). In 1 Timothy 2:5, Paul declares that "there is one God and one mediator between God and men, the man Christ Jesus."

In addition, Scripture also declares that human nature is so sinful that people are utterly hopeless apart from Jesus.[11] The New Testament affirms the importance of hearing the gospel and believing, as, for example, in Peter's message at the first Pentecost (Acts 2) and Jesus' Great Commission (Matt. 28:19 – 20).

---

10. For example, see John 1:29 and 20:30 – 31.
11. Again, see Romans 3.

Now, pluralists have their ways of dealing with biblical passages like these, and inclusivists have some techniques of their own as well. We will look at these methods later. The important point for now is that we can easily understand how and why Christians from the very inception of their faith have traditionally regarded exclusivism as an essential part of the total Christian message.

## EXCLUSIVISM AND THEOLOGICAL CONSIDERATIONS

Besides the clear teaching of the New Testament, Christian exclusivists find natural support in a number of related theological ideas. A short list of these interconnected doctrines includes the deity of Christ, the Incarnation, the Atonement, and the Resurrection. If Jesus Christ is the eternal Son of God who became human for the express purpose of dying, and if he died as an atonement for human sin and then rose bodily from the grave, it is difficult to see how anyone can believe it is possible for some people to attain salvation apart from him. It is precisely because pluralists like John Hick see the logical entailments among these Christian doctrines that they exert such effort to deny them. To be a pluralist is unthinkable apart from a repudiation of the doctrinal heart of the historic Christian message.

John Hick admits to a logical connection between exclusivism and such Christian doctrines as the deity of Christ:

> There is a direct line of logical entailment from the premise that Jesus was God, in the sense that he was God the Son, the Second Person of the Divine Trinity, living in a human life, to the conclusion that Christianity, and Christianity alone, was founded by God in person; and from this to the further conclusion that God must want all his human children to be related to him through his religion which he has himself founded for us; and then to the final conclusion, [that] "Outside Christianity, [there is] no salvation." [12]

Hick is certainly right in observing that if anyone accepts Christian doctrines such as these, that person is logically

---

12. John Hick, *God Has Many Names* (Philadelphia: Westminster, 1982), 58.

committed to accepting Jesus Christ as the only Savior. As we
will see, Hick's rejection of Christian exclusivism logically requires him to reject these essential Christian beliefs.

## EXCLUSIVISM IN NON-CHRISTIAN RELIGIONS

Christian exclusivism receives an enormous amount of criticism in academic and ecclesiastical circles these days. But
Christians are not the only exclusivists in the world. Most religions are exclusivist in the sense that each regards its own tradition's central claims as true and competing claims as false. If
anyone doubts this, all one needs to do is share the Christian
gospel with some Muslim or Hindu and observe what happens.

It is ironic that when religious exclusivism gets savaged
these days, one seldom, if ever, finds the self-professed guardians
of religious "tolerance" and "open-mindedness" criticizing the
many non-Christian exclusivists in the world. I am not quite sure
what to make of this except possibly that some people are really
more anti-Christian than they are anti-exclusivist.

## SOME OTHER FACETS OF EXCLUSIVISM

A full account of Christian exclusivism should take note of
several other convictions. One of these is the belief that unevangelized mature persons[13] will not only experience God's judgment,
but deserve such. Yet it is important to remember that Christian
exclusivists often disagree greatly about the nature of hell and the
condition of the lost. Opponents of exclusivism almost always
ignore these disagreements and represent all exclusivists as
advocates of the most extreme views on the subject of hell.

Another aspect of exclusivism that will require more comment later is the belief held by almost all exclusivists that

---

13. My language here intentionally omits mentally incompetent persons and
children who die before reaching a level of maturity that would allow them to
grasp the full import of the gospel, including the fact that they are sinners in
need of God's forgiveness. This is another subject that is treated later in the
book.

human destiny is fixed at the moment of physical death.[14] The attainment of Christ's redemption requires that people trust in Christ before death.

A significant disagreement between exclusivists and inclusivists involves the possible role of general revelation in salvation. Inclusivists insist that people outside any sphere of Christian influence may nonetheless be saved by trusting in whatever they may learn from God's general revelation in Creation, conscience, and history. Exclusivists disagree.

Bruce Demarest identifies in the Puritan view of general revelation several points that are shared by most exclusivists. General revelation, Demarest explains,

> teaches no redemptive truths. But if general revelation . . . provides insufficient light for the salvation of the soul, it does nevertheless serve at least two practical ends. In the first place, general revelation leaves the unrepentant sinner without excuse. Objectively, the divine self-disclosure in Creation, history, and conscience is sufficiently clear that God should be known as Creator, Ruler, and Judge.[15]

The apostle Paul notes in Romans 1 how humans willfully rebel against the light that God gives them in nature, history, and conscience. In Demarest's words, Paul "proceeds to establish the link between rejection of the witness of general revelation and man's guiltiness. Since all people are brought face-to-face with the light of God in Creation, providence, and conscience, all are morally responsible for the rational choices they make. Since all people plainly see the signature of God written on His works, no pleas of ignorance can be offered."[16] This helps explain why all humans are "without excuse" (Rom. 1:20).[17]

---

14. I discuss a possible exception to this claim in chapter 10.

15. Bruce A. Demarest, *General Revelation* (Grand Rapids: Zondervan, 1982), 69–70.

16. Ibid., 246.

17. Demarest identifies a second purpose of general revelation that is irrelevant to our discussion. General revelation, he writes, also "serves as a necessary prolegomenon to the divine special revelation. The evidence of Creation, history, and conscience establish[es] a necessary point of contact between the sinner and the gospel. In Puritan thought, general revelation relates to special revelation as the foundation of a building to the superstructure. When God addresses man with His

This leads Demarest to conclude that

> General revelation thus performs the function of rendering man judicially accountable before God. If God were not discernible in His works, if general revelation were invalid or failed to mediate knowledge of God, then the masses of people who have never heard the gospel would be innocent of their ungodliness and irreligion. But since knowledge of God is mediated to all by general revelation, human accountability to God is firmly established. Hence in practice, general revelation becomes a vehicle not for salvation but for divine judgement.[18]

This position is totally rejected by pluralists, who believe that non-Christian religions are equally legitimate vehicles for salvation, and by inclusivists, who insist that the content of general revelation is sufficient to bring unevangelized people to salvation in the total absence of information about the Christian gospel.

## EXCLUSIVISM AND ITS OPPONENTS

If Christian exclusivism is true, then all the following alternatives are false:

1. Atheism

2. Universalism

3. Non-Christian Religions

4. Pluralism

5. Inclusivism

Because this book focuses on the dispute among exclusivists, pluralists, and inclusivists, we will not discuss atheism.

In one sense, the broad topic of universalism is also beyond the scope of this book, even though many pluralists such as John Hick are also universalists. By "universalism," I mean the belief

---

saving message in the living and written Word, man recognizes Him as God on the grounds of His preliminary universal disclosure" (*General Revelation*, 70).

18. Ibid., 246.

that no human being will ultimately be lost. Sooner or later, universalists believe, God will eventually save every person. We will refer to universalism later only in connection with some observations as to why Christian inclusivists tend to reject the position.

This book will also say very little about the specific content of various non-Christian religions. I have intentionally given this book a narrow focus. It would require a quite different book, probably twice as long as this one, to examine specific details of non-Christian religions. My focus in this work is on positions 4 and 5 on my list, pluralism and inclusivism.

## PLURALISM

A pluralist is a person who thinks humans may be saved through a number of different religious traditions and saviors. John Hick explains his own pluralism this way: "There is not merely one way but a plurality of ways of salvation or liberation . . . taking place in different ways within the contexts of all the great religious traditions." [19]

Hick, whose many writings on the subject set the pace for many Western pluralists, wants to avoid a relativism that treats all religious beliefs and systems equally. He has proposed a test that enables us to grade religions, and as he sees things, at least the major religions of the world pass this test. All qualify equally as valid roads to salvation. However, movements such as the Peoples' Temple of Jim Jones and the Branch Davidian cult of David Koresh fail the test, as do systems that practice human sacrifice or cannibalism. Unfortunately, pluralists have not identified a criterion to mark the line between authentic and inauthentic "responses to the Transcendent" clearly enough to make it work on a broad scale. Even though Hick tells us that Jim Jones was on the wrong side of the line, it will not be clear to everyone how to apply the same criterion in other cases. [20]

---

19. John Hick, *Problems of Religious Pluralism* (New York: St. Martin's Press, 1985), 34.

20. I owe this point to Doug Geivett of Talbot Theological Seminary.

But Hick and other prominent pluralists do not think that the salvific value of the great religions requires anyone to believe in the existence of the myriad gods found in these systems. That would only commit pluralism to what amounts to a new religion, namely, a new type of polytheism with a confusing and contradictory amalgam of beliefs. As Joseph Runzo explains, sophisticated pluralists hold "that there is only One Ultimate Reality, but that Ultimate Reality is properly, though only partially, understood in different ways." [21] (A bit later, when we hear pluralists like Hick tell us that God or Ultimate Reality is unknowable, I will ask the reader to reflect a bit on how the pluralist can *know* the content of propositions like Runzo's.)

## INCLUSIVISM

Inclusivists agree with exclusivists and differ from pluralists in affirming that Jesus Christ is the only Savior. No man or woman can possibly be saved apart from the redemptive work of Jesus Christ, inclusivists say, and this is so whether the person is raised under a Christian, Buddhist, Muslim, or Hindu system.

But inclusivists also part company with exclusivists, a point that at first may seem confusing. How can a position that insists on the deity of Jesus Christ and the indispensability of his redemptive work for salvation be a source of concern to theologically conservative Christians?

One way to answer this question is to introduce two technical terms that inclusivists frequently use. They distinguish between the *ontological necessity* of Christ's work as redeemer and the separate claim that Christ's redemptive work is *epistemologically necessary.*

The word *ontology* refers to what is the case in the world of being or reality. Inclusivists affirm the ontological necessity of Christ's redemptive work; they agree with exclusivists that Jesus' atoning work is the necessary ground for the salvation of

---

21. Joseph Runzo, "God, Commitment, and Other Faiths: Pluralism vs. Relativism," *Faith and Philosophy* 5 (1988): 351.

any human being. The word *epistemology* points to an entirely different matter, that of what people know or believe. When inclusivists deny the epistemological necessity of Christ's work, they are saying that it is not necessary for people to *know* about Jesus or *believe* in Jesus to receive the benefits of his redemptive work.

So inclusivists believe that salvation is impossible apart from Jesus and that he is the only Savior. But this does not mean that people have to know about Jesus or actually believe in him to receive that salvation. There are problems, inclusivists argue, in limiting salvation to those who have a conscious knowledge of and explicit faith in Jesus Christ. What do we do with the millions of people, past and present, who never heard the gospel? Is God's grace limited to the relatively few who, often through accidents of time and geography, happen to have responded to the gospel?[22] Isn't it reasonable to think that millions of others over the long course of human history would have believed had only they known? Inclusivists dismiss exclusivists as cold, uncaring people who are unwilling to explore other ways to expand the scope of God's love.

Many people find this kind of emotional appeal persuasive. Of course, exclusivists reject the way they and their beliefs are stereotyped. Exclusivists also think it is important to consider some other information before allowing one's feelings to dictate Christian doctrine.

Many inclusivists appear to have more respect for pluralism than for exclusivism. In some cases, as we will see, they suggest that if they ever found reasons to abandon their inclusivism, they would move toward pluralism and away from exclusivism.[23]

----

22. Ken Gentry, Jr., of Christ College has pointed out in personal correspondence that this was an early objection to the exclusivism of Christianity. Such pagan critics of Christianity as Porphyry (A.D. 232 – 303) and Julian the Apostate (A.D. 332 – 363) drove this objection home frequently. See Robert J. Wilken, *The Christians as the Romans Saw Them* (New Haven: Yale University Press, 1984), 162, 180.

23. For samples of this troubling insinuation, see Clark Pinnock, "Toward an Evangelical Theology of Religions," *Journal of the Evangelical Theological Society* 33 (1990): 362; and John Sanders, *No Other Name* (Grand Rapids: Eerdmans, 1992), 106.

According to inclusivist Clark Pinnock, exclusivists "have made it ridiculously easy for liberals to attack classical theology (in particular, its christology). Scholars such as John Hick have been making mincemeat out of us [evangelical Christians], arguing all too convincingly that evangelicals have nothing to contribute to the discussion of religious pluralism."[24] Few of us enjoy being reduced to mincemeat. When we examine the pluralist's case against exclusivism, we will have to see whether the complaints of John Hick and other pluralists are as powerful as Pinnock seems to think.

## CONCLUSION

This chapter has introduced the three positions we will examine in this book. They can be distinguished in terms of their response to the following two propositions:

(1) Jesus Christ is the only Savior.

(2) No one can be saved unless he or she knows the information about Jesus' person and work contained in the Gospel and unless he or she exercises explicit faith in Jesus Christ.

Pluralists, as we now know, reject both (1) and (2). Inclusivists accept (1) but reject (2). And exclusivists affirm both (1) and (2). The major question I will seek to answer in the rest of this book is whether pluralists or inclusivists have produced arguments strong enough to justify the repudiation of exclusivism, which is the position of historic Christianity. I believe the reader will discover a host of reasons to embrace Christian exclusivism.

---

24. Clark Pinnock, foreword to John Sanders, *No Other Name,* xiv.

# PART ONE

# PLURALISM

Chapter Two

# THE EARLY STAGE OF JOHN HICK'S PLURALISM

Our discussion of pluralism centers on the work of John Hick, who is generally acknowledged to be the best-known and most influential proponent of pluralism today.

Other writers have analyzed the development of Hick's thought over the past forty years,[1] so I will focus on the two major stages in the evolution of his pluralism. This chapter will examine the earlier stage of his thinking, extending roughly from 1970 to 1980; chapter 3 will explore the changes his thinking has undergone since 1980. It is important to see that Hick's pluralism did not suddenly appear in a mature, fully developed form. It first took root and then grew, sometimes fitfully, as Hick tried first one thing and then another to make his evolving view of pluralism work. Tracing some of these steps can be instructive.

The second stage of Hick's pluralism marked a major break with elements of his earlier position. In fact, the reason that Hick developed his second stage was because his first attempt at pluralism was, to my mind, a dismal failure.[2] Understanding the

1. See Gavin D'Costa, *John Hick's Theology of Religious Pluralism* (Lanham, Md.: University Press of America, 1987), and Paul R. Eddy, "John Hick's Theological Pilgrimage," *Proceedings of the Wheaton College Theology Conference* (1993), vol. 1, *The Challenge of Religious Pluralism: An Evangelical Analysis and Response,* 26 – 38.

2. Hick himself would reject my judgment on the matter and contend that his current views are for the most part continuous with what he wrote in the 1970s. Readers will have an opportunity to make their own judgments on this matter.

mistakes of the first stage will make it easier for us to reach a judgment about the value of stage two.

## JOHN HICK'S COPERNICAN REVOLUTION

During the early 1970s John Hick regarded his approach to world religions as so radical that he began to describe it as a Copernican Revolution in religion. As Hick saw things, Christian exclusivism is analogous to the old, outdated Ptolemaic model of the solar system. Claudius Ptolemy, an astronomer and mathematician who lived in Alexandria, Egypt, from around A.D. 100 to 170, taught what is called the geocentric theory of the solar system and pictured the sun and the planets as revolving around the earth. Ptolemy's view was challenged by the heliocentric, or sun-centered, theory proposed by the Polish astronomer Nicolaus Copernicus (1473 – 1543). For several hundred years now, it has become almost a cliché that scholars who have a dramatically new idea to propose describe it as a "Copernican Revolution."

However, Hick was doing more than just suggesting that his theory was revolutionary. He found in the Copernican Revolution an appropriate metaphor for his own new understanding of the relation between the major religions of the world. That is, Hick's proposal in comparative religions was patterned after the transformation from a Ptolemaic model to a Copernican model in cosmology.[3]

Hick sees Christian exclusivism as analogous to the outdated Ptolemaic model of the solar system. He defined Ptolemaic *theology* as a system "whose fixed point is the principle that outside the church, or outside Christianity, there is no salvation." [4] Unfortunately, when worded in this way, Hick's definition suggests significant bias against Christianity, because exclusivism can be found in many religions.

Hick's self-described Copernican alternative to Ptolemaic theology involved the removal of Christianity from any exalted

---

3. I owe my formulation of this point to Doug Geivett.
4. John Hick, *God and the Universe of Faiths* (reprint, London: Collins, 1977), 125.

or exclusive place at the center of the world's religions. Just as Copernicus replaced the earth-centered paradigm with a sun-centered model, so Hick proposed to replace the historic Christian view that Jesus Christ is the center of the religious world with the claim that God is the center. The historic Christian position that there is no salvation apart from Jesus Christ must now be abandoned, according to Hick. His substitute sees all the world religions rotating around God, not Jesus.

### The Notion of Epicycles

Many students of astronomy are surprised to learn how well the old Ptolemaic model worked in explaining the apparent motion of the planets. The reason for its success depended on the skill of Ptolemaic astronomers in designing what are called *epicycles.* An epicycle was an orbit on an orbit, such as the orbit of the moon around the earth, which in turn is orbiting around the sun. There were times when the Ptolemaic astronomers could only explain certain motions of heavenly bodies by postulating orbits on orbits on orbits, as seen in the following diagram.

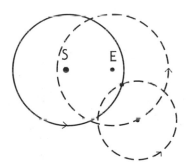

For several years after Copernicus proposed his competing model of the solar system, Ptolemaic astronomers continued to do a better job of explaining and predicting the movement of the planets. Eventually, astronomers recognized that the successes of the Ptolemaic model were due to a mistake in Copernicus's thinking. Copernicus believed the planetary orbits were circles. After Johannes Kepler showed convincingly that planetary orbits are elliptical, the power of the Copernican system to explain the solar system became evident.

Ever since, the epicycles of the old Ptolemaic theory have served as an example of arbitrary and contrived theorizing, not based on evidence, adopted solely to enhance the plausibility of the theory. While the repeated addition of more and more epicycles made it possible to preserve the Ptolemaic system a bit longer, the whole enterprise became increasingly cumbersome and complex. The Copernican model was eventually adopted because it was simpler and less cumbersome.

According to John Hick, the religious analogue of Ptolemaic astronomy is any view that places Christianity at the center of the world's religions. Hick denigrates attempts (whether by exclusivists or inclusivists) to protect Christianity from the challenge of the world's religions by comparing them to the epicycles of the Ptolemaic system. That is, the efforts of exclusivists and inclusivists to defend their positions are examples of contrived, arbitrary, and artificial measures. Their efforts are not prompted by an honest attempt to conform theory to evidence, but are merely tinkering with one's model so as to continue delaying its inevitable demise.

## Why Was Hick's "Revolution" Necessary?

Although we will look more closely later at Hick's reasons for his self-described "revolution," a brief look at some of them now will be helpful for understanding what Hick was thinking in the early 1970s. One reason was Hick's growing awareness of saintly and holy people in non-Christian religions.[5] As one observer explains, Hick's encounters with devout and moral non-Christians led him to think it was no longer possible to "argue that Christianity or Christ is the sole means of salvation since it is evident that many outside Christianity, and outside the influence of the historical Jesus, are in fact saved."[6]

But does encountering pious, devout, and even saintly non-Christians prove the truth of pluralism? As we will see, certain

---

5. See the early pages of John Hick, *God Has Many Names* (London: Macmillan, 1980).

6. D'Costa, *John Hick's Theology of Religious Pluralism*, 48.

assumptions underlie Hick's response to these encounters. One of these is Hick's dubious claim that the apparently contradictory truth-claims found in different religions are not what they seem.

During the first stage in the development of his pluralism, Hick also appealed to the notion of an all-loving God. He believed that the existence of an all-loving God required the rejection of any "Ptolemaic" version of Christianity; by this he rejected any form of Christian exclusivism. The more Hick thought about it, the more convinced he became that a loving God would not exclude *anyone* from his salvation.

Ironically, Hick himself provided the major reason why this line of thinking had to be rejected. Hick recognized that pluralism could not succeed if any specific knowledge about God is possible. Suppose we knew, for example, that personal monotheism is true. We could then know that polytheism and pantheism are false. But if we know that pantheism is false, then we can hardly continue to view pantheistic systems as paths to God that function on an equal footing with theism. And so we find Hick conceding that God as he (or whatever) really is, is unknowable.

But when Hick then appeals to the love of God as the ground of one of his convictions, he is clearly contradicting himself. A loving God is a supreme being with known properties. As soon as we can legitimately ascribe any properties to God, problems arise for the pluralist, specifically because *that* God with *those* attributes (such as love) will conflict with the gods of other religious systems who do not possess those attributes or that set of properties.

Hick has been criticized for attempting to have it both ways. On the one hand, he promoted a pluralistic, non-Christian approach to the world religions while, on the other hand, all his talk about a loving, personal God sounded a lot like Christianity. If, as Hick insists, no one can have any knowledge about God, then no one can know that the Supreme Being is a loving God. But if we cannot know *this*, then we can hardly use information that we cannot know — that God is love — as the basis of an attack on exclusivism. It took Hick quite a while to see why he could not continue to appeal to divine love in his arguments for pluralism.

Hick also argued that religious beliefs are typically a result of geographic and cultural conditioning. Someone born in Dallas, Texas, is most likely going to be a Christian. Guess what that person would be if born in Sri Lanka, Mecca, Tokyo, Tehran, or New Delhi? A just and loving God would hardly punish people for what is basically an accident of birth. But again we see how difficult it is for Hick to avoid this essentially self-defeating line of thinking. The argument falters unless he can free his appeal to geographic and cultural conditioning from references to divine love.

These reasons cited by Hick as support for the first stage of his pluralism are only mentioned in passing now, but it is not too soon for the reader to begin thinking about the strengths and weaknesses of Hick's early arguments.

### Summary

John Hick reached a point in his life where he rejected Christian exclusivism, a position he compared to the old Ptolemaic theory of the universe. He ridiculed any effort to rescue a Christ-centered system (either exclusivist or inclusivist) as an epicycle, that is, a purely arbitrary move that only revealed the desperation of the old-time view of Christian superiority.

Hick's own alternative to a Christ-centered view of religion was his so-called Copernican Revolution. This amounted to a proposal to remove Jesus Christ and Christianity from the center among the world's religions and replace them with "God." Hick was convinced that his new pluralism would be more tolerant than Christianity and would allow other religions to achieve an equal standing with the Christian faith.

## PROBLEMS WITH HICK'S FIRST STAGE

Hick's movement away from important aspects of his early pluralism was hardly an accident. He changed his position on some issues because it became clear he had to. An examination of Hick's reasons for changing his mind provides some interesting insights regarding both Hick and his pluralism.

We noticed how Hick's Copernican Revolution had removed Jesus from any central place in relation to the world's religions and replaced him with an all-loving God. Hick failed to appreciate that many non-Christian religionists would regard his appeal to an all-loving God as an insult or, even worse from Hick's standpoint, as a new kind of exclusivism. These people saw clearly how Hick was still operating under the influence of a "narrow" Judeo-Christian type of thinking. To be all-loving, the God operating at the center of Hick's system would have to be a *personal* God. But many religious systems express belief in a nonpersonal Supreme Principle; others neither affirm nor deny the existence of a personal God.

Hick ascribed not only personality to his God, but also biblical attributes such as love. This created a dilemma. If the "God" of his new theocentric approach to religion were personal, then Hick would appear guilty of excluding nonpersonalistic views of God (pantheism). But if, by contrast, he opted for a nonpersonal God at the center, then he would be excluding religions such as Christianity, Judaism, and Islam that understand God as personal. Since one of his objectives was tolerance as opposed to "closed-minded Christians," it did not work to appear intolerant toward anyone.

All this was embarrassing for another reason. It suggests that Hick knew in advance what he wanted his conclusions to be and was simply cutting the cloth to fit the customer. Was not Hick simply churning out his own arbitrary, ad hoc epicycles? He who had set himself up as the radical revolutionary rejecting such evils as exclusivism, intolerance, and epicyclic imaginings appeared to be guilty of those very sins. Clearly he had to do something.

Hick set about to extricate himself from the dilemma. First, he tried arguing that God was both personal and impersonal, as though this would make his system large enough to include theists, pantheists, and everyone else he wanted. But a little reflection showed how unsatisfactory that move was. The world contains some square objects and some round objects, but it does not and cannot contain objects that are round and square at the same time. Likewise, reality might contain a personal God or an impersonal god, but it is logically impossible for God to be both personal and impersonal at the same time.[7]

### Hick's Unknowable God

In the midst of this, Hick was also denying that human beings could know God. God, he wrote, "exceeds all human thought." [8] At the time, in 1973, denying the knowability of God had assumed the status of an initiatory rite into the mysteries of neo-liberal theology.[9] So it is unclear whether Hick's adoption of theological agnosticism was anything more than a less-than-thoughtful surrender to the liberal *zeitgeist.* Eventually, however, the unknowability of God would prove to be a key step in his attempt to rescue his Copernican Revolution from all kinds of difficulties.

What Hick failed to see, however, is that his affirming God's unknowability only created new problems. Let us reflect a bit. Hick tells us that God is unknowable. But in making this claim, Hick reveals at least two things that he knows about God. For one thing, he seems to know that there is a God. Second, to claim that God is unknowable is already to know something very significant about God. If God really were unknowable, then we should be unable to know that he is unknowable.

Hick faced another difficulty. There are two reasons why God might be unknowable. First, his (or its) nature has not been revealed to us. In this case, people could only worship an unknown "God" in ignorance (Acts 17:23). That is not very reassuring. Second, perhaps God has no attributes, but in this case,

---

7. The ruminations of so-called Process Theologians do not contradict this claim since the bi-polar god so many of them talk about has two poles to his being, one personal and the other impersonal. That kind of thinking generates different problems. See Ronald Nash, *The Concept of God* (Grand Rapids: Zondervan, 1983) and Ronald Nash, ed., *Process Theology* (Grand Rapids: Baker, 1987).

8. John Hick, *God and the Universe of Faiths* (London: Macmillan, 1973), 178.

9. For examples, see Ronald Nash, *The Word of God and the Mind of Man* (Phillipsburg, N.J.: Presbyterian and Reformed, 1992), chaps. 1 – 3.

Hick's God would turn out to be like the *nirguna Brahman* of Hinduism. Theologian D. Forrester has concluded that Hick's ideas would be acceptable only to followers of the Vedanta strain of Hinduism.[10] But if this were so, Hick's early theory would have had the ironic consequence of replacing Christian exclusivism with the view of a particular Hindu sect. So Hick's thought did not quite constitute a revolution. He would only have replaced one alleged Ptolemaic position with one of his own.

In one of his most recent books Hicks states that "the Buddhist concept of *sunyata* in one of its developments, namely as the anti-concept excluding all concepts, provides a good symbol for the Real [that is, God in itself]."[11]

Philosopher Doug Geivett thinks there is more to these hints that Hick is really the advocate of a variant of Eastern religious thought. He writes:

> As it turns out, Hick's affinity with the Eastern thread of religious history is partly constituted by his religious pluralism. Historically, pluralism is antagonistic to the core principles of Christianity. But syncretism and pluralism have been prominent features of Eastern thought for centuries. Conceptually, it is clear that Hick is much more at home with Eastern models of religious reality than with the tradition into which he was, as he says, born. (Hick's own example just goes to show how potentially irrelevant it is to to the final outcome of one's faith, especially in the contemporary world, where one is born or how one is brought up.)[12]

Geivett, Forrester, and others who have drawn attention to this often-overlooked aspect of Hick's thought have identified a serious problem. In a later chapter we will encounter Hick's challenge to what he calls "the myth of Christian uniqueness."

---

10. D. Forrester, "Professor Hick and the Universe of Faiths," *Scottish Journal of Theology* 29 (1976): 69.

11. John Hick, *An Interpretation of Religion* (New Haven: Yale University Press, 1989), 246.

12. R. Douglas Geivett, "John Hick's Approach to Religious Pluralism," *Proceedings of the Wheaton College Theology Conference* (1993), vol. 1, *The Challenge of Religious Pluralism: An Evangelical Analysis and Response*, 49.

We have encountered in the last section of this chapter a different myth, something we could call "the myth of Hick's neutrality."

## CONCLUSION

How Hick eventually tried to escape the problems he created for himself in the 1970s is discussed in chapter 3. But it seems clear that Hick's first attempt at a Copernican Revolution was a philosophical and theological disaster. Instead of this pluralism flowing logically from a set of plausible premises, the reverse seems to have been the case. Hick started with a conclusion and then sought premises to support it. The opponent of a Ptolemaic-type exclusivism had snared himself in his own version of it; the self-described enemy of theological epicycles had invented his own.

Chapter Three

# THE SECOND STAGE
# OF HICK'S PLURALISM

Stage one of Hick's evolving pluralism was his move from a Christ-centered approach to religion to a God-centered model. During the 1980s Hick moved from this theocentric theory to a salvation-centered model. One way to approach these changes in Hick's thinking is to notice some elements that he borrowed from the eighteenth-century philosopher Immanuel Kant.

## HICK AND THE PHILOSOPHY OF IMMANUEL KANT

Hick came under the influence of Kant's philosophy during graduate studies at the University of Edinburgh. Interestingly, Kant had described his own theory of knowledge as a Copernican Revolution in philosophy. Kant's "revolution" attacked the usual way philosophers had thought about human knowledge before he came along.[1] In Kant's terms, the prevailing picture of human knowledge had placed reality at the center of the knowing process.[2] Humans attained knowledge when their thinking accommodated itself to the structure of reality. In

---

1. I have argued that Kant's claims in this regard are exaggerated and ignore at least one major predecessor, St. Augustine of Hippo (A.D. 354 – 430). See Ronald Nash, *The Light of the Mind: St. Augustine's Theory of Knowledge* (Lexington, Ky.: University Press of Kentucky, 1969).
2. This sentence obviously must not be understood in any literal way. It extends the image of the earth at the center of the solar system.

this pre-Kantian theorizing, reality was paramount and human knowledge was derivative or dependent.

Kant changed all this by theorizing that the human mind was at the center of the knowing process. Knowledge of the world depended on the fundamental structure of the human mind. Once the real world that lies beyond human consciousness begins feeding us sensory information such as colors, sounds, tastes, and smells, the mind organizes and relates this information in various ways. Our knowledge of the world is therefore a product of two factors, information received through the senses and the organizing powers of the human mind.

This new way of looking at things required Kant to distinguish between the way the world appears to us (the phenomenal world) and the way the world really is (the noumenal world).[3] The so-called phenomenal world is the world as it appears to human consciousness; these appearances necessarily reflect the organizing powers of the human mind. The world that appears to us is not necessarily the way the world really is; it is more correct to think of the phenomenal world as a product of the ways our mind forces us to conceive it. All this points to another world "behind" the world of appearance; this is, for Kant, the real world or, in his phrase, the *noumenal world*.

This noumenal world exists independently of our consciousness. A little reflection reveals why, for Kant, the noumenal world must be both unknown and unknowable. After all, the only way we can attain knowledge of the real or noumenal world is if we can somehow free ourselves from the controlling influence that our minds have on knowledge. Of course, that is impossible.

Basic to Hick's move to a second stage of pluralism is his distinction between the phenomenal God and the noumenal God. In Hick's words, "This is the familiar distinction, classically drawn by Immanuel Kant, between something as it is in

---

3. For a more complete account of Kant's theory, see Ronald Nash, *The Word of God and the Mind of Man* (Phillipsburg, N.J.: Presbyterian and Reformed, 1992), chap. 2. Also see Ronald Nash, "Gordon Clark's Theory of Knowledge," in *The Philosophy of Gordon H. Clark*, ed. Ronald H. Nash (Philadelphia: Presbyterian and Reformed, 1968), 141–47.

itself, a *Ding an sich,* and that same thing as humanly perceived, with all that the human mind contributes in the process of perception." [4] Hick believes the distinction is justified because of the many different and sometimes conflicting ways that the real God (the noumenal God) appears to people in the different religions (the phenomenal God). All of the phenomenal concepts of God we encounter in the religions of the world are misleading and inadequate. What we should be seeking is God as it, he, or she is in itself.

## THE UNKNOWN GOD OF JOHN HICK

Hick also suggests that we drop the word "God" from our religious language. The old term is simply too loaded with connotations that remind people of specific religions. Instead of "God," Hick talks of *Reality* or the *Real* or *Ultimate Reality.* Hick defines "the Ultimate" as

> that putative reality which transcends everything other than itself but is not transcended by anything other than itself. The Ultimate, so conceived, is related to the universe as its ground or creator, and to us human beings, as conscious parts of the universe as the source both of our existence and of the value or meaning of that existence.[5]

It should be obvious that with this approach Hick is attempting to get away from the mistakes he made in the first stage of his pluralism, which often found him operating with elements of an older, more theistic, even Christian concept of God. A serious pluralist does not want to do that.

The earlier Hick was admired for his ability to talk about complex philosophical and theological theories in a clear way. The older Hick seems to have lost some of that skill. He summarizes his newer way of thinking about God as follows: "The divine presence is the presence of the Eternal One to our finite human consciousness, and the human projects are the culturally

---

4. John Hick, *Disputed Questions in Theology and the Philosophy of Religion* (New Haven: Yale University Press, 1993), 158.
   5. Ibid., 164.

conditioned images and symbols in terms of which we con-
cretize the basic concepts of deity." [6]

This is a rather tortured way of saying that human beings
need finite anthropomorphic images or pictures that will help
direct their minds toward the infinite unknowable divine reality.
Different religions provide us with different images and symbols. Even though all these pictures are culturally conditioned
(and thus distorted), they nonetheless help followers of these religions to reach a more definite understanding of God.
Moreover, Hick thinks, these culturally conditioned images have
the *Ultimate Reality* as their source.

We are never aware of God as God really is, Hick advises,
since "that would be equivalent to perceiving the world as it is
unperceived." [7] Rather, we are aware of God

> as God is thought of and experienced through the conceptual
> "lens" of our own tradition. For each tradition functions as a
> kind of mental "lens" — consisting of concepts, stories (both
> historical and mythical), religious practices, artistic styles,
> forms of life — through which we perceive the divine. And
> because there is a plurality of such "lenses" there is a plural-
> ity of ways in which God is concretely thought and experi-
> enced.[8]

We should note here that Hick is precluded from saying
that he *knows* any of these points. After all, it would be an obvious contradiction to say, as Hick does, that God is unknowable
and then proceed to describe God as "the Eternal One." Hick
evades this contradiction by treating all his comments about the
Ultimate as hypotheses. Even if God is unknowable, he contends, it is nevertheless plausible to believe that something Real
stands behind the various religious experiences, and that the
Real is essentially the same thing experienced in different, even
conflicting, ways.[9] However, one observes that Hick's confident
assertions about God lack any thing resembling the tentative-
ness that usually accompanies hypothetical musings.

---

6. John Hick, *God Has Many Names* (Philadelphia: Westminster, 1982), 53.
7. Hick, *Disputed Questions*, 159.
8. Ibid.
9. See ibid., 178.

Hick's earlier pluralism saw him wrestling with a God who was both personal and impersonal. Hick's distinction between the phenomenal God and the noumenal God helped him escape his dilemma. He began to make the quite different claim that the Real or Ultimate could be authentically thought of and experienced as both personal and nonpersonal.[10]

Believers in religions such as Christianity, Judaism, and Islam perceive the Real as personal, whereas believers in some other religions perceive the Ultimate as impersonal. None of these concepts gives us the Real as it really is. Instead, each results from the Real affecting different people within the contexts of differing religious traditions. But, Hick continues, we cannot say that the Real

> is personal or impersonal, one or many, active or passive, substance or process, good or evil, just or unjust, purposive or purposeless. No such categories can be applied, either positively or negatively, to the noumenal. Thus, whilst it is not correct to say, for example, that the Real is personal, it is also not correct to say that it is impersonal — nor that it is both personal and impersonal, or neither personal nor impersonal. All that one can say is that these concepts, which have their use in relation to human experience, do not apply, even analogically, to the Real *an sich* [in itself].[11]

In other words, Hick states that among the things we cannot know is whether God is good or evil. Such a disclaimer is inevitable, given Hick's necessary skepticism about the Real as it is in itself. But we should remember this claim when Hick talks about how the Real is involved in all the authentic religions that bring men and women to salvation. The test of salvation turns out to be Hick's major device in eliminating inauthentic religions, such as the cults of Jim Jones and David Koresh. But once it becomes clear that we lack all awareness of whether the Real is good or evil, who is to say that an evil cult may not function as an authentic response to the Ultimate?

Hick's claim that we may "authentically" think of the Real as both personal and nonpersonal is puzzling. Hick's adverb

---

10. See John Hick, "The Theology of Pluralism," *Theology* 86 (1983): 337.
11. Hick, *Disputed Questions*, 177.

implies that these personal and nonpersonal conceptions and experiences are true in some way. One has the nagging feeling that Hick really thinks he can figure out what the Unknowable Real is really like, even if no one else can. Furthermore, all this knowledge about the unknowable God functions as the basis for his rejection of the knowledge claims of Christianity. Each reader will have to decide if Hick really is operating on two different levels — sometimes acting as though he is simply setting forth hypotheses, and at other times as though he has a confidence about these things that borders on what we usually call knowledge.

Hick goes a step further when he writes that "the very plurality and variety of human experiences of the Real provide a wider basis for theology than can the experience of any one religious tradition taken by itself."[12] This seems like an odd thing to say. Hick is claiming that a large number of conflicting experiences, all of an unknown God whom we shouldn't even call "God," are somehow supposed to bring us closer to a more accurate understanding of that which is essentially unknowable.

Hick tells us that no predicates can be applied to the Real. This means that we cannot say that God is loving or all-knowing or all-powerful or holy or a spirit or a person. We cannot say that God is good or evil. Is it not natural, then, to suppose that Hick's words for God have no significant content? Once we have unpacked the ramifications of Hick's radical theological skepticism in this way, David Basinger wonders why we should not hold instead "that there is no higher Reality beyond us and thus all religious claims are false — i.e., why not opt for naturalism? Or why not adopt the exclusivistic contention that the religious claims of only one perspective are true?"[13] When you begin by stating that point $A$ in your system is the recognition that humans cannot know anything about God, how can you rationally get from point $A$ to point $B$ — or anywhere, for that matter?

---

12. John Hick, "Towards a Philosophy of Religious Pluralism," *Neue Zeitschrift für Systematische Theologie under Religionsphilosophie* 22 (1980): 146.
13. David Basinger, "Hick's Religious Pluralism and 'Reformed Epistemology': A Middle Ground," *Faith and Philosophy* 5 (1988): 422.

## HICK'S CRITERION FOR GRADING RELIGIONS

Another question arises in connection with the second stage of Hick's pluralism: Does Hick's position mean that we are stuck with every religion humans have followed — no matter how evil or absurd — or are there criteria by which religious systems can be graded? Some religions have practiced human sacrifice and cannibalism. The pivotal sacrament in the Jim Jones cult involved drinking Kool-Aid laced with strychnine. Does an acceptance of pluralism require us to treat every religion as equally valid? Hick responds no and proposes that religions be graded in terms of how they measure up to the criterion of "salvation."

Two observations are in order here. First, Hick's move clearly indicates that he does not believe that all religions are equal. Some religions are better than others, and some "religions" may be unworthy of support. Second, Hick's insistence on a test to grade religions does not mean that the followers of inadequate religions will be lost. Hick is not only a pluralist, but also a universalist. Ultimately and eventually, every member of the human race will be saved. This salvation will encompass even the worst moral monsters of history, including Adolf Hitler and the Nazis, Joseph Stalin and his secret police, and the entire gamut of serial killers, rapists, child molesters, and the like.

In his book *An Interpretation of Religion*, published in 1989, Hick states that

> the great world faiths embody different perceptions and conceptions of, and correspondingly different responses to, the Real from within the major variant ways of being human; and that within each of them the transformation of human existence from self-centeredness to Reality-centeredness is taking place. These traditions are accordingly to be regarded as alternative soteriological "spaces" within which, or "ways" along which, men and women find salvation/liberation/ultimate fulfillment.[14]

The threefold expansion of "salvation" into "salvation/liberation/ultimate fulfillment" suggests that Hick is going to explain salvation in a *very* broad way.

---

14. John Hick, *An Interpretation of Religion* (New Haven: Yale University Press, 1989), 240.

Hick maintains that the great world religions share a common concern with salvation "which identifies the misery, unreality, triviality, and perversity of ordinary human life, affirms an ultimate unity of reality and value in which or in relation to which a limitlessly better quality of existence is possible, and shows the way to realise that radically better possibility." [15] The differences between what one finds in Christianity and other religions "are variations within different conceptual schemes on a single fundamental theme: the sudden or gradual change of the individual from an absorbing self-concern to a new centering in the supposed unity-of-reality-and-value that is thought of as God, Brahman, the Dharma, Sunyata or the Tao." [16]

What Hick calls "salvation" assumes different forms in the different major religions. Within Christianity, for example,

> the concrete reality of salvation is the transformation of human existence from a sinful and alienated self-centeredness to a new centering in God, revealed in Christ as both limitless claim and limitless grace. The [Christian] experience of salvation is the experience of being an object of God's gratuitous forgiveness and love, freeing the believer to love his and her neighbour.[17]

Once we turn from Christianity to consider the other major religions, it quickly becomes apparent how elastic the notion of "salvation" is as a criterion for grading religions. For example, in Buddhism Hick explains, "the salvific human transformation is understood as liberation from the powerful illusion of 'me' or 'self.'"[18] The many varieties of the family of Indian religions that Western scholars came to call Hinduism offer three paths to liberation: (1) a path of spiritual insight by which I realize that I am identical with the Universal Self;[19] (2) salvation by action or doing or living a particular kind of life;[20] and (3) the way known as *bhakti*, which Hick explains as "self-giving devotion to the

---

15. Ibid., 36.
16. Ibid.
17. Ibid., 46 – 47.
18. Ibid., 41 – 42.
19. Obviously, this path is pursued within a pantheistic framework. The technical term for it is *jnana-marga*.
20. The technical term is *karma-marga*.

Real encountered as the divine Thou," which takes the form "of loving devotion to a divine Lord and Saviour."[21]

Islam creates a few problems in Hick's search for some view of salvation/liberation/ultimate fulfillment in each of the major religions. As Hick explains,

> Islam does not use the concept of "salvation" and does not think of the human condition in terms of a "fall" involving a guilt and alienation from God that can only be cancelled by a divine act of atonement. However, the Qur'an does distinguish radically between the state of *islam* — a self-surrender leading to peace with God — and the contrary state of those who have not yielded themselves to their Maker and who are therefore in the last resort enemies of God.[22]

We must keep in mind that this rapidly expanding set of examples of salvation/liberation/ultimate fulfillment constitutes the test by which Hick will discriminate between authentic and inauthentic religions.

### An Initial Critique of Hick's Use of Salvation

It is reassuring to see that Hick realized his need for some criterion to grade religious systems. Without it, his pluralism would appear a bit ridiculous, since he would end up endorsing a host of foolish or evil systems as equals with the major world religions. But his criterion is too elastic and vague.

Once one identifies salvation as the ultimate test of a genuine religion, everything begins to turn on how "salvation" is defined. Consider the options:

> If salvation is the attainment of illumination, then Buddhism can save.

> If salvation is union with a Universal Self, then Hinduism can save.

> If salvation is forgiveness and justification, then Christianity can save.

---

21. Hick, *An Interpretation of Religion*, 39.
22. Ibid., 48.

If salvation is maintaining a proper relation to one's ancestors, then Shintoism can save.

But if salvation is defined as overthrowing an oppressor class and establishing a classless society, why can't we say that communism can save as well? Did not those systems that practiced child-sacrifice or mutilation or cannibalism also offer what they thought was salvation? Did not Jim Jones offer his followers salvation? Is not Hick's appeal to salvation so vague and general that he ends up offering a kind of religious supermarket with countless paths to salvation? Of course, Hick tries to avoid this kind of chaos by insisting that all legitimate forms of salvation exhibit one common trait, namely, a movement from a state of self-centeredness to Reality-centeredness. But how does Hick arrive at this particular concept of salvation? He claims that he derives it from a careful investigation of the major religions. As we will see later, this is questionable in that his procedure requires him to ignore anything that weakens his thesis and obliges him to introduce considerable distortion into almost every religion he discusses.

Hick's propensity to oversimplify becomes apparent once we remember that the world's religions not only understand the Ultimate differently (for some of these religions, there is no Ultimate), but also differ in their understanding of the basic human predicament and the means by which humans are delivered (saved) from this predicament. Harold Netland asks,

> Is the human predicament brought on by sin against a righteous and holy God, or is it due to *maya* (illusion) and *avidya* (ignorance)? Is salvation to be thought of in terms of justification before God or in terms of liberation from *samsara*? It is highly misleading to speak as if all religions share a common soteriological goal and simply differ on the means to reach it.[23]

Hick's criterion simply will not work until it becomes possible to determine the truth or falsehood of assorted major beliefs taught by each religion. According to Netland,

> Christianity can only be considered effective in providing salvation as justification if the human predicament is in fact

---

23. Harold A. Netland, *Dissonant Voices* (Grand Rapids: Eerdmans, 1991), 160.

characterized by alienation from God due to human sin and if God has in fact made possible through Jesus Christ justification of sinful humanity. Similarly, Theravada Buddhism can only be said to be effective in providing liberation if the human condition is in fact one of ignorance concerning the true nature of reality combined with a bondage to craving and desire, and if strictly following the Noble Eightfold Path will indeed bring the elimination of craving and thus *nirvana*. In other words, a given religion can be regarded as soteriologically effective only if its diagnosis of the human condition is accurate and if its proposed way for achieving the intended soteriological goal will indeed bring about the desired effect.[24]

As much as he might like to try, Hick cannot escape the pivotal question of truth. This important issue will be the subject of the next chapter.

## An Exception to Hick's Transformation of Self-Centeredness

On pages 52 – 55 of his *Interpretation of Religion,* Hick admits to a bizarre exception to his previous statements about salvation. To fully appreciate what happens on these pages, one must see Hick's move against the backdrop of several contemporary developments in theology, in Western society, and in many centers of American higher education. These developments include what is called *liberation theology,* whose advocates reduce Christianity to a movement to eradicate poverty and oppression. What is problematic is the tendency of liberation theologians to care only about the poor and oppressed people who interest them and to seek to address the issues of poverty from an unabashed and unrepentant Marxist perspective.[25]

What is called *feminist theology* (or even better, *feminist liberation theology*) often links up with powerful segments of the liberationist movement and what still passes for Marxism these

---

24. Ibid., 160 – 61.
25. See Humberto Belli and Ronald Nash, *Beyond Liberation Theology* (Grand Rapids: Baker, 1992). See also, Ronald Nash, ed., *Liberation Theology* (Grand Rapids: Baker, 1988); Ronald Nash, *Poverty and Wealth* (Dallas: Probe, 1992); and Ronald Nash, *Social Justice and the Christian Church* (Lanham, Md.: University Press of America, 1990).

days.[26] Feminist theology contends that the historic Christian faith must be repudiated as a haven for patriarchal sexism that oppresses women even as "capitalism" according to the Marxist view oppresses the poor.[27] Both liberationist Marxism and feminist Marxism extend their power in American society through the political correctness movement that now holds captive many American institutions of higher learning.

Hick shows that he passes the political correctness test, but in the process raises doubts about his analysis of salvation and the consistency of his thought. Hick begins his discussion by noting how many feminist theologians object to his analysis of salvation as a repudiation of self-centeredness. Hick assures us that these feminist thinkers "are today contributing major and sometimes startling insights which it would be a serious mistake for others to ignore." [28] One such "insight" from the feminists turns out to be their challenge to Hick's thesis that salvation is a movement away from self-centeredness to Reality-centeredness. Hick cites St. Augustine (and Augustine's analysis of sin as pride or self-assertion) as one ancient source for his understanding of salvation.

Hick explains the source of the feminist's discomfort with all this: "The feminist critique of this strand of Christian thought is that self-assertion is not the basic human temptation but rather the characteristic *male* temptation; and that its female counterpart, within the existing patriarchal world cultures, is different." [29]

In the politically correct world of the radical feminist, the attitudes of pride and self-assertiveness define what feminists think is *good*, at least for feminists. While pride and self-assertiveness are basic sins for men, the proper female analogue to male pride (man's defining sin) is female timidity, sentimen-

---

26. For more on the mutations of Western Marxism, see Ronald Nash, *The Closing of the American Heart* (Dallas: Probe, 1990), chap. 9.

27. For an account of how radical feminism substitutes a new pagan religion for historic Christianity, see Ronald Nash, *Great Divides* (Colorado Springs: NavPress, 1993), chap. 3.

28. Hick, *An Interpretation of Religion*, 52.

29. Ibid.

tality, triviality — in short, all the attributes that radical feminists associate with passive women in a male-dominated society.

To reduce a long, incredible concession to political correctness to its bottom line, Hick admits that female salvation may well be the opposite of male salvation. Female salvation, at least for oppressed and male-dominated women, is the transformation from weakness to self-centeredness!

So Hick, who, I contend, sometimes misrepresents the content of major religions when it advances his thesis, is now willing to redefine the central concept of his later system (salvation) when faced with the risk of offending militant, radical feminists.

Perhaps out of embarrassment, Hick attempts to put his glaring inconsistency in a better light by suggesting that not all women have weak egos. So perhaps for them, his more usual analysis of "sin" might still hold. In Hick's own words,

> In so far as anyone, female or male, lacks the ego-development and fulfillment necessary for a voluntary self-transcendence, the prior achievement of self-fulfilled ego may well be necessary for a true relationship to the Real. For in order to move beyond the self one has first to *be* a self. This means that the contemporary woman's liberation movement, as a part of the larger movement for human liberation, is in the front line of salvific change in our world today.[30]

## CONCLUSION

It is evident that John Hick saw the need to move beyond the serious inadequacies of his first version of pluralism, even if he has refused to acknowledge these defects. The problems that afflict his second version are more difficult to uncover. Simply put, this is because, like the Ptolemaic astronomers of old, every time Hick is confronted by a difficulty, he takes another step backward into an epicycle. His distinction between the phenomenal gods and the noumenal God only serves to plunge him into serious conceptual difficulties. His appeal to salvation as the

---

30. Ibid.

essential core of the major religions works only when he over-simplifies or distorts his data from these religions.

In all of this, we must remember that this collection of confusions is Hick's alternative to historic Christian theism. Hick's reasoning obviously has appeal for many people in the academic world, most notably those who are already biased against an exclusivist religion. It may also appeal to people with a sentimental bent whose emotions are affected by what they can understand from Hick's contemporary prose. But some will conclude that what Hick does best is show the power that an anti-Christian ideology can have.

Chapter Four

# REASON, TRUTH, AND RELIGIOUS PLURALISM

Read carefully the following statements by pluralist thinkers:

1. John Hick claims that exclusivism rests uncritically on Aristotelian notions of truth, where truth "is essentially a matter of either-or. It is either this or not this: it cannot be both."[1]

2. Wilfred Cantwell Smith thinks that exclusivism is based on an outdated and Western view of the law of the excluded middle: either $A$ is true or non-$A$ is true. In Smith's words, "[I]n all ultimate matters, truth lies not in an either-or but in a both-and."[2]

3. Paul Knitter writes that "all religious experience and all religious language must be two-eyed, dipolar, a union of opposites."[3]

Each of these statements appears to be an all-out assault on the usual role that logical thinking is presumed to have in responsible thought and action. Paul Knitter, for example, appears to link pluralism with a repudiation of logical categories of

---

1. John Hick, "A Philosophy of Religious Pluralism," in *The World's Religious Traditions: Current Perspectives in Religious Studies. Essays in Honour of Wilfred Cantwell Smith, ed.* F. Whaling (Edinburgh: T. & T. Clark, 1984), 164.

2. Wilfred Cantwell Smith, *The Faith of Other Men* (New York: New American Library, 1963), 17.

3. Paul Knitter, *No Other Name? A Critical Survey of Christian Attitudes Toward the World Religions* (Maryknoll, N.Y.: Orbis, 1985), 221.

thinking that leads some people to reason that if Christianity is true, then non-Christian forms of faith must be false.

W. C. Smith also eschews either-or thinking in religion in spite of the irrationality that follows when we ignore either-or thinking anywhere else in life. Consider the statement "either this mushroom is poisonous or it is not." Turning this either-or into a both-and could be fatal in ways that transcend logic. Whatever Smith's theory turns out to mean, he clearly contradicts the common-sense position that the truth of Christianity implies the falsity of other religions.[4] The above quote from John Hick places him squarely in the same company. These statements from leading pluralists raise the issue of where they stand with respect to reason and truth in religion.

## PLURALISM AND THE LAWS OF LOGIC

One of the fundamental laws of logic is the principle of the excluded middle. Stated formally, this principle says that "Either *A* [some proposition] is true or *A* is false." One example of the law of the excluded middle is "Either Ross Perot will be the next President of the United States or Ross Perot will not be the next President of the United States." Any proposition having this form is necessarily true. But contrast that statement with this one: "Ross Perot will be the next President of the United States and Ross Perot will not be the next President of the United States." Any proposition having this second form — a form that is inconsistent with the law of the excluded middle — must be false.

The law of non-contradiction exhibits the form "A [something that exists] cannot be both B and non-B at the same time in the same sense." Any proposition that attributes contradictory properties to some subject at the same time and in the same sense must be false.

I suspect that John Hick, W. C. Smith, and Paul Knitter avoid violating these logical principles whenever they deal with nonreligious issues. But do their earlier statements really

---

4. See Smith, *The Faith of Other Men*, 92 – 131.

suggest that religion is one area of life where the laws of logic are not necessary? Are Hick, Smith, and Knitter religious irrationalists? If the quotations we cited are any indication, they certainly seem to be.

If pluralists really object to exclusivism because of its reliance on such logical laws as the principle of the excluded middle or the law of non-contradiction, pluralism is in serious trouble. This would mean that in their view of things, any one who would become a pluralist must first abandon the very principles of logic that make all significant thought, action, and communication possible.[5] As Harold Netland argues, "[T]he price one must pay for rejecting the principle of non-contradiction is simply too high." He explains,

> The price of rejecting the principle of noncontradiction is forfeiture of the possibility of meaningful affirmation or statement about anything at all — including statements about the religious ultimate. One who rejects the principle of noncontradiction is reduced to utter silence, for he or she has abandoned a necessary condition for any coherent or meaningful position whatsoever.[6]

This path leads to nothing less than intellectual suicide. Hick and the other pluralists surely do not want to make the repudiation of logic an essential feature of pluralism. To uncover what they *do* mean, however, will require a shift to the separate but related issue of truth.

## PLURALISM AND THE QUESTION OF TRUTH

Christians believe that the proposition "Jesus Christ is God Incarnate" is true. Muslims believe that the proposition "Jesus Christ is not God Incarnate" is true. According to the pluralists' statements, these two propositions should not be viewed as

---

5. For reasons of space I must resist the strong temptation to explain all this in detail here. I have done so, however, in *The Word of God and the Mind of Man* (Phillipsburg, N.J.: Presbyterian and Reformed, 1992), chap. 10, and in *Worldviews in Conflict* (Grand Rapids: Zondervan, 1992), chap. 4.

6. Harold Netland, "Exclusivism, Tolerance and Truth," *Missiology* 15 (1987): 84 – 85.

contradictory. Because we are giving these pluralists the benefit of the doubt and assume they are not rejecting the laws of logic, we must seek another way to understand their conviction that both these beliefs about Jesus are true.

### What Is Truth?

The first thing to note about truth is that it is a property of propositions. To say that *x* is a property of something is to mean that *x* is a characteristic, feature, or trait of that thing. Just as baldness is a property of some men and redness a property of some roses, so truth is a property of some propositions.

What is a proposition? It is a statement in which the predicate affirms or denies something about the subject. Understood in this way, propositions are different from other uses of language such as commands (statements like "Close the door") and expressions of emotion (the reaction of someone who has just hit his thumb with a hammer). Examples of propositions are the following: "The door is closed" or "Ron Nash is the world's greatest living golfer"[7] or "Reformed Theological Seminary has a campus in Orlando, Florida."

Propositions may have a number of different properties. Propositions may be long or short, simple or complex. They may also be true *or* false. The word *or* (another appearance of the principle of the excluded middle) is important in the preceding sentence. No proposition may be *both* true *and* false in the same sense and at the same time. One way we can identify a false proposition is if it asserts a contradiction, as in the statement "Some bachelors are happily married men." Because the word *bachelor* means an unmarried man, the foregoing proposition is logically contradictory and thus necessarily false. One way we can identify a true proposition is whether it describes the way things really are. If I state, for example, that on April 20, 1993, the Orlando Magic basketball team had a record of forty-one wins and forty-one losses, we can easily check to see whether the claim is true. It is true if the team really had that number of wins and losses; otherwise it is false.

---

7. This proposition serves as a reminder that many propositions are false.

Some people want to use the word *truth* as a property of things other than propositions. For example, "Michael Jordan is a true shooting guard" or "That lady is wearing a true fur coat"[8] or "Joe Smith is a true friend."[9] As we will discover, pluralists appeal to such usage as part of their way of reconciling what appear to be conflicting religious beliefs. I will argue, however, that all of these other usages of the word *true* are dependent upon its primary sense as a property — not of basketball players or fur coats or friends, but of propositions.

### Propositions and Beliefs

Propositions are related to acts of believing. When someone says that he believes that such and such is the case, the "such and such" is always a proposition. To say that I believe that today is Friday is equivalent to saying that I believe the proposition "Today is Friday" is true.

Philosophers often distinguish between two kinds of believing, *belief that* and *belief in*. In *belief that,* my act of believing is directed toward some proposition. But in *belief in,* my act of believing is directed toward a person. If I believe in my friend, Joe Smith, it means that I trust him. When I believe in God, it means that I trust God and have committed myself to him. It is very important to see that *belief in* presupposes *belief that.* If I believe in God, it is because of all the propositions about God that I believe are true.[10]

The apparently conflicting beliefs of the different world religions, I will argue, all make unavoidable reference to logically contradictory propositions affirmed by the followers of these religions. It is the pluralists' rejection of this claim that contains the key to understanding their apparent repudiation of logic in the quotations provided. The pluralist simply denies that appar-

---

8. The contrast here is with an artificial fur coat.
9. The contrast here is with a friend who sometimes fails to do things we expect friends to do.
10. For a full argument in defense of this important claim, see Ronald Nash, *Christian Faith and Historical Understanding* (Dallas: Probe Books, 1984), chap. 8.

ently conflicting truth-claims are really truth-claims; he or she thinks that they will turn out to be something different.

## THE PLURALIST'S NEW UNDERSTANDING OF RELIGIOUS TRUTH-CLAIMS

So far we have learned that pluralists think that what we usually take to be the truth-claims of the world's great religions are not really contradictory. This is not because pluralists (at least the ones examined in this book) reject the laws of logic, but because they deny that what look like truth-claims really are. Because the statements are something other than cognitive truth-claims, they turn out to complement, not contradict, each other. In 1981, Hick tried to explain all this by saying that the supposed truth-claims of competing religions are in fact "linguistic pictures or maps of the universe, whose function is to enable us to find salvation/liberation, the limitlessly better quality of existence that the nature of reality is said to make possible."[11]

A major influence on Hick's thinking about this issue has been Wilfred Cantwell Smith, from whom Hick learned to oppose the older view of religions as competitive systems of belief or mutually incompatible systems.[12] Because of Smith's influence on pluralist thinking about truth, we must briefly survey his position.

### *W. C. Smith and Rejection of Propositional Truth in Religion*

W. C. Smith argues that the notions of truth and falsity should not be applied to religion.[13] It is wrong, he contends, to think of Christianity as true and Islam as false.

> Christianity is not true absolutely, impersonally, statically; rather, it can *become* true, if and as you or I appropriate it to ourselves and interiorize it, insofar as we live it out from day

---

11. John Hick, "On Grading Religions," *Religious Studies* 17 (1981): 461.

12. See John Hick, foreword to *The Meaning and End of Religion* by W. C. Smith (New York: Harper & Row, 1978), ix – xviii.

13. Smith, *The Meaning and End of Religion*, 322.

to day. It becomes true as we take it off the shelf and person-
alize it, in actual experience.[14]

For Smith, exclusivism errs in making *beliefs* (and therefore
propositions as well) an essential feature of religious traditions.
This easily leads to a misleading distinction between true and
false beliefs. It no longer makes sense to ask which religion is
truest, Smith believes.

Smith distinguishes between what he calls the "cumulative
tradition" of a religious community and the faith of the individual believer. While the tradition is external and objective, the believer's faith is internal and subjective. The tradition is "the
entire mass of overt objective data that constitute the historical
deposit, as it were, of the past religious life of the community in
question."[15] Creeds and codes that nourish the faith of individual people are an important part of this tradition. Faith, by contrast, is Smith's way of referring to "an inner religious experience
of involvement of a particular person. . . . [It is] the impingement
on him of the transcendent, putative or real."[16] Faith refers to the
way a person feels and lives when encountering transcendence.
Basic, then, to Smith's new view of religious truth is the claim
that we should stop concentrating on the idea of "religion" and
focus instead on external cumulative traditions and internal
faith.

It takes a long time for the external cumulative tradition to
form. Typically, when one thinks of a religion such as Hinduism
or Christianity, it is this tradition that is in view. But Smith contends that the subjective faith of the individual believer is far
more important than the external tradition.

One important consequence of Smith's theory is its effect on
doctrines, rituals, and the like, which henceforth possess only
secondary importance. The propositional truth that some people
still view as important resides in the cumulative tradition. But
because primary importance attaches to inward faith, propositional truth must become secondary.[17]

---

14. W. C. Smith, *Questions of Religious Truth* (London: V. Gollancz, 1967): 67 – 68.
15. Smith, *The Meaning and End of Religion*, 141.
16. Ibid.
17. See ibid., 153.

All this leads Smith to think that religious "truth" differs considerably from the kind of truth we encounter in everyday life. Instead of being propositional, religious truth is *personal;* it must have an existential impact on the life of the believer. It transforms and changes the person's life. The cumulative traditions of this or that religion *become* true as they transform the lives of individual believers within that tradition.[18] Smith considers it misleading to talk about the supposed truth of Christ's resurrection as though this were objective, static, and merely propositional. Christ's resurrection only becomes true insofar as it transforms individual people. Hence, no religion is true in the objective or propositional sense. But all religions are true subjectively! And of course, this personal, subjective view of religious truth ends up implying that the same religious claim (proposition) can be true for me and false for you. It also implies that a religious proposition that was false for me yesterday can *become* true tomorrow.

### An Evaluation of Smith's Position

Does not Smith's position still involve a repudiation of logical principles such as the law of non-contradiction and the law of the excluded middle? It is obvious that Smith thinks it does not. The "truth" that interests Smith is not related to the propositions that are part of the external traditions; it is rather a function of the purely subjective attitudes and feelings of different people. When religious "truths" are nonpropositional, they cannot contradict other nonpropositional "truths."

I find several difficulties in Smith's position:

1. Smith's position leads to several absurd consequences. Consider the different ways that broccoli affects people. While less dramatic perhaps than some religious issues, broccoli has been known to have an existential or transforming effect on some people. Imagine a dispute between two people, one of whom is former U.S. President George Bush. The other person is a professional nutritionist whom we will call Violet Jones.

---

18. See W. C. Smith, *Towards a World Theology* (Philadelphia: Westminster, 1981), 187.

Ms. Jones utters the proposition "Broccoli is good," while George Bush denies her proposition. Do we have a contradiction here? Not really, because — extending Smith's analysis of religious "truth" to this case — Ms. Jones is really uttering the subjective judgment "I like broccoli" while President Bush is really saying, "I do not like broccoli." The reason that the two utterances are not contradictory is because each is describing something different. Ms. Jones's words are doing nothing more than describing *her* feelings on the subject, while President Bush's words are describing *his* feelings. There is no contradiction; both statements are true at the same time.

Although W. C. Smith's way of handling religious "truth" might appear to solve a serious problem for pluralists (the problem created by their apparent rejection of logic), it only raises new and equally troubling questions. For one thing, Smith's position on religious "truth" entails that no two people ever really disagree over religious truth-claims. After all, Ms. Jones and President Bush are not really disagreeing; each is simply describing a personal preference. Do pluralists really mean to say that the many apparently serious disagreements over religious claims are reducible to trivial disputes over different subjective states?

In addition, Smith's position implies that no two people ever mean the same thing when they utter the same religious proposition. Two people could sing a duet to the famous words "Jesus loves me, this I know." But because, according to Smith, what is important in this context is the subjective, existential impact the propositions have and because subjective impacts differ considerably from person to person, the vocalists would in fact be singing about two different things. The soprano might be singing about the effect of Jesus's love on *her* subjective states while the alto might be referring to what is occurring in *her* subjective consciousness.

Finally, Smith's theory of religious truth entails that no religious claim can ever be false; all of them are true, in Smith's sense of the word. When a Christian affirms the deity of Christ, he is honestly reporting the subjective effect that his belief has on him. When a Muslim denies the deity of Christ, he is honestly reporting what is occurring in his subjective religious conscious-ness. Neither person is wrong. How wonderful! Or how ironic that religious pluralism is bought at such a high price. If Smith is right, then almost every follower of the world's major religions is wrong in his or her understanding of what is going on in that religion.

2. Smith's approach ignores the fact that in addition to ex-pressing personal feelings and the like, adherents to a religion are always making cognitive assertions in propositions that have some presumed objective truth value. This point has been well-stated by Stephen T. Davis, a philosopher at the University of Claremont and a former colleague of John Hick.

> Of course, theological propositions do not exhaustively ex-plain a religion; we must look to what might be called prac-tice as well as theory. Perhaps Smith means that a religion is "true" if, say, its adherents practice it sincerely, or if their lives are morally admirable, or if the religion automatically "works" for them. If he does mean something like this, he is right that the truth of Christianity does not entail the falsity of, say, Buddhism or Islam. But this is hardly to refute the no-tion that there is a broad propositional or theological element in religion.[19]

This leads Davis to conclude that "The fact that for some person Christianity has *become truth* (in Smith's sense) is quite unrelated to what I am calling the *truth or falsity of Christianity,* that is, the truth or falsity of its crucial claims."[20]

Smith's highly eccentric theory of religious "truth" turns out to be irrelevant to the concerns of most religious believers in the world. As difficult as it might be for Smith to sway tradition-alist Christians to his view, there are also millions of Muslims, Hindus, and Buddhists out there who will oppose his theory as strenuously as Christians, and for good reason. For his theory to work, Smith must redefine and in the process distort a huge set of propositions that all these people believe and regard as essen-tial to their so-called tradition and their personal faith.

---

19. Stephen T. Davis, "Evangelicals and the Religions of the World," *Reformed Journal* (June 1981): 11.
    20. Ibid.

3. Finally, the pluralist's subordination of propositional truth to private, personal truth has the relation between the two completely wrong. Smith holds that the fundamental sense of truth is personal and private and that the objective, propositional type of truth is derivative. A little reflection will quickly show that the fundamental sense of truth that underlies any other use of the term is propositional.

Harold Netland summarizes Smith's understanding of personal truth as follows: "[I]n religion, truth is to be understood primarily as personal, that is, as having its locus in persons who satisfactorily appropriate religious beliefs."[21] For convenience, suppose we call this summary of Smith's position S.

Now, Netland asks, does Smith expect the rest of us to accept his S as true? Surely so. But S can only be true in the sense of propositional truth because, Netland continues,

> S expresses a proposition which makes a claim about reality; it asserts that reality is such that truth is primarily personal and has its locus in persons who satisfactorily appropriate religious beliefs. And in proposing S Smith is suggesting that we accept it because it is *true*, that is, that reality actually is as the proposition expressed by S asserts it to be.[22]

If the truth of S were only personal and subjective, then that "truth" would depend upon someone's appropriating it, upon S's affecting my life in some way. But this would mean that S could be true for Jones, but not true for Nash. Yet Smith could never allow for the relativity of S. He presumes that S is true for everyone. But this then means that S's truth reflects the propositional sense of truth.

Once again we find the pluralists submerged in quicksand. Each time they attempt to escape from one problem, they seem to end up landing in another difficulty. Sometimes, the later problems encountered are far worse that the earlier ones. In this case Smith ignores how wise people will only appropriate beliefs subjectively if they think those beliefs are true in the propositional sense.[23]

---

21. Netland, "Exclusivism, Tolerance and Truth," 90.
22. Ibid.
23. For a detailed defense of this claim, see Nash, *Christian Faith and Historical Understanding*, chap. 8.

To say that "Allah is a righteous judge" is true would then be to recognize that a particular Muslim's life and conduct is congruous with belief that Allah is a righteous judge. But this presupposes that the Muslim accepts and appropriates not only a set of practices and a manner of life but also a set of beliefs and values which taken together articulate a comprehensive perspective on reality. And such beliefs will be accepted in the first place because the Muslim regards them as true, [namely,] as accurately portraying the way reality actually is. Thus personal truth should not be regarded as an alternative to propositional truth, for it presupposes propositional truth.[24]

All this leads Netland to a very important conclusion: "Smith seems to be confusing the question of truth with that of response to the truth. . . . But the truth value of a belief or proposition and the degree to which one allows that belief to impact upon one's life are two very different things."[25] While beliefs and propositions are not equivalent, and while belief certainly includes more than mental assent to a proposition, belief always includes believing *something*, and that something is a proposition. Belief may be more than mental assent, but it cannot be less. "The fact is," Netland concludes, "that adherents of the various religions believe certain propositions about the religious ultimate, humanity, and the nature of the universe to be true. And where these beliefs conflict — as they occasionally do — we have the problem of conflicting truth-claims."[26]

### John Hick and the Rejection of Propositional Truth in Religion

John Hick takes a similar approach as W. C. Smith to the apparent conflict among the truth-claims of the world religions. Smith linked doctrines and other religious propositions to external traditions and then subordinated these traditions to the more important subjective faith of individual believers. Hick transforms religious doctrines into myths, or pictures, that help direct humans toward the infinite, unknowable, divine reality.[27] Hick's

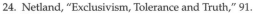

24. Netland, "Exclusivism, Tolerance and Truth," 91.
25. Ibid.
26. Ibid.
27. See John Hick, *God and the Universe of Faiths* (London: Macmillan, 1973), 178 – 79.

reduction of religious beliefs and doctrines to myth is totally for-
eign to the way most religious devotees understand their faiths.
Moreover, it suffers the same logical fate as W. C. Smith's theory.
Harold Netland explains,

> [M]ythological statements about the Real are only informa-
> tive to the extent that they are parasitic upon nonmythologi-
> cal-literal-truth. For the question whether any given behavior
> or pattern of life (loving one's neighbor, fasting regularly, sac-
> rificing children to Moloch) is to be regarded as an appropri-
> ate response to the Real will depend upon our ability to
> formulate clearly certain propositions about the nature of the
> Real and our relationship to the Real.[28]

Hick's claim that myths become true to the extent that they
produce appropriate responses to the Real on the part of believers is indistinguishable from W. C. Smith's theory. Hick is attempting to escape the clutches of logical rules such as the law
of non-contradiction. He attempts this by redefining religious
truth in a nonpropositional way, which makes his theory susceptible to the same criticisms that make Smith's similar views so
untenable.

## WHAT SHOULD NON-CHRISTIANS THINK
## OF THE SMITH-HICK THEORY OF RELIGIOUS TRUTH?

Through almost everything he writes about pluralism, John
Hick leaves the impression that the people he most hopes will
accept his views are the recalcitrant Christian exclusivists of the
world. He leaves little doubt that he regards this Christian recalcitrance as a product of ignorance, prejudice, intolerance, and no
small amount of cultural conditioning — all defects that Hick
himself presumes to be free of.

There is merit in recognizing that many non-Christians
have their own good reasons to reject Hick's work. This is certainly the case with Hick's handling of the issue of propositional
truth in other religions.

---

28. Harold A. Netland, *Dissonant Voices* (Grand Rapids: Eerdmans, 1991), 221.

As Harold Netland explains, pluralism is committed "to the position that the many different conceptions of the divine or religious ultimate (Allah, Shiva, Krishna, Yahweh, Nirvana, Sunyatta, etc.) are all various culturally and historically conditioned images of the same single divine reality. This entails that [all these terms] ultimately have the same referent, although the connotations of the respective terms may differ."[29]

Netland notes the implausibility of this stance. Consider the different meanings these names for the ultimate have in the traditions to which they belong. For example, Netland writes, "the ontological implications of the Judaeo-Christian image of the divine as Yahweh, who is ontologically distinct from, and independent of, the created world, are incompatible with the ontological monism of the notion of Nirguna Brahman from Advaita Vedanta, or the monistic idealism of the Yogacara school of Buddhism."[30]

It defies common sense to suppose that the people who uttered all the competing claims we find in the major religions believed they were doing anything other than truly describing the nature of reality. Not only are the things they say apparently truth-claims to our minds, but also they were understood to be truth-claims by the people who uttered them. Basic to Hick's approach to the world religions is the conviction that regardless of what the followers of these religions thought they were doing, pluralists know better. This is hardly convincing as a foundation for interreligious tolerance. It is also a highly questionable method of hermeneutics. Hick's assumption on this point is indefensible both historically and hermeneutically.

Netland has even stronger words of criticism for pluralism.

> It is difficult to escape the conclusion that [Hick's] resolute desire to resolve the problem of conflicting truth-claims without admitting that some beliefs of some traditions are false has driven him to a radical reinterpretation of religious beliefs and doctrines in mythological terms. The price for resolving the problem in this manner, however, is that Hick's theory must be called into question as a general explanation

29. Netland, "Exclusivism, Tolerance and Truth," 86.
30. Ibid.

of the nature of religious experience. For his understanding of religious beliefs bears little resemblance to that of most believers in the major traditions and consequently will be vigorously resisted by all within the mainstream of these traditions.[31]

It simply will not do to downplay, ignore, or minimize the serious and very real differences among the world religions. They do conflict logically. In his book *Dissonant Voices,* Netland explores and documents at some length the logical incompatibilities among Hinduism, Buddhism, Islam, and Shintoism with special reference to three questions: What do these religions teach about the nature of the religious ultimate? about the nature of the human predicament? and about the nature of salvation or enlightenment or liberation?[32]

It is not plausible, Netland argues, "to maintain, as many do today, that the different religions all make essentially the same claims and teach basically the same truth." On the contrary, he states,

> Careful examination of the basic tenets of the various religious traditions demonstrates that, far from teaching the same thing, the major religions have radically different perspectives on the religious ultimate, the human predicament, and the nature of salvation. Any attempt to produce an essential unity in outlook among the many religions will result in distorting at least some of the actual religious beliefs of followers of the various traditions.[33]

A number of specialized books provide additional support for Netland's claim.[34]

The major religions conflict at the level of essential doctrine. The pluralist claim that doctrinal disputes are irrelevant because they have little or nothing to do with salvation flies in the face of

31. Netland, *Dissonant Voices,* 231. Netland provides several examples on pp. 231 – 32.

32. Ibid., 36.

33. Ibid., 37.

34. See Ninian Smart, *The Religious Experience of Mankind,* 3d ed. (New York: Scribner's, 1984); David S. Noss and John B. Noss, *A History of the World's Religions,* 8th ed. (New York: Macmillan, 1990); and W. B. Comstock, ed. *Religion and Man: An Introduction* (New York: Harper & Row, 1971).

the evidence. Most religions insist that correct believing is a necessary condition for salvation. This is certainly true in the case of Christianity (Acts 16:31 and John 3:16). Parallels to this can also be found in non-Christian religions.[35]

World religions also conflict at the level of the kinds of conduct they advocate. Not surprisingly, Netland maintains that "the common assumption that all religions ultimately are teaching the same things in their own culturally conditioned ways is *prima facie* untenable. Not only are they not all saying the same things, but the particular issues addressed in the various religions are not necessarily the same."[36] According to William Christian, attempts to play down the major disagreements among the world's religions by suggesting that they all teach pretty much the same thing "seem very implausible, and certainly much current talk in the aid of these views is loose and sentimental."[37]

With all this as background, it is hard to deny that the world's major religions contain some false teaching. Naturally, Muslim or Buddhist exclusivists will think the errors are to be found in systems other than their own. Moreover, the millions of non-Christians in the world will not be satisfied with the distortions that pluralists like Hick and Smith introduce into their beliefs.

## CONCLUSION

We must keep in mind that the tortuous moves that pluralists such as John Hick and W. C. Smith make in matters pertaining to truth and logic are made necessary by their rejection of exclusivism and their claims that pluralism is intellectually superior. We contend that any theory that so mishandles truth and logic cannot stand.

---

35. See Netland, *Dissonant Voices,* 232.
36. Ibid., 111.
37. William A. Christian, *Oppositions of Religious Doctrines: A Study in the Logic of Dialogue Among Religions* (London: Macmillan, 1972), 5.

Chapter Five

# PLURALISM AND THE CHRISTIAN UNDERSTANDING OF JESUS CHRIST

John Hick recognizes the importance of the orthodox Christian understanding of Jesus Christ to the pluralism-exclusivism debate. He writes, "If Jesus was literally God incarnate, and if it is by his death alone that men can be saved, and by their response to him alone that they can appropriate that salvation, then the only doorway to eternal life is Christian faith. It would follow from this that the large majority of the human race so far have not been saved."[1] If Jesus really is God and if his atonement is the only ground of human salvation, then pluralism must be false.

Hick contends that

There is a direct line of logical entailment from the premise that Jesus was God, in the sense that he was God the Son, the Second Person of the divine Trinity, living in a human life, to the conclusion that Christianity, and Christianity alone, was founded by God in person; and from this to the further conclusion that God must want all his human children to be related to him through his religion which he has himself founded for us.[2]

1. John Hick, "Jesus and the World Religions," in *The Myth of God Incarnate,* ed. John Hick (London: SCM, 1977), 180.
2. John Hick, *God Has Many Names* (Philadelphia: Westminster, 1982), 58.

Hick here uses a well-known form of logical reasoning that assumes the following form:

If *A*, then *B*

*A*

*Therefore, B*

Whenever the first clause (*A*) of a true hypothetical statement is true, then the second clause (*B*) must be true.[3] For example, consider the true hypothetical statement, "If Pierre is guillotined, then Pierre will be dead." If the first clause is true, then the second is also true and Pierre is in deep trouble. Consider now a different hypothetical statement: "If the historic Christian understanding of the person and work of Christ is true, then human salvation depends upon a proper relationship to Jesus Christ." If the first clause of our new hypothetical statement is true, then pluralism is in deep trouble.

Hick recognizes that he has no choice. He must do everything possible to attack the truth of the first clause (concerning the person and work of Christ). He must use every weapon at his disposal to deny such Christian doctrines as the deity of Christ, the Incarnation, and the Trinity.

In this chapter we will examine the major steps in Hick's attempt to destroy Christian confidence in the high view of Jesus that has characterized historical and orthodox Christianity from its inception. I will lay out, largely without comment, Hick's theories about what Jesus said and believed about himself, about how the church supposedly deified Jesus over a long period of time, about why the doctrine of the Incarnation is nothing but a myth, and about the alleged uniqueness of Christ and Christianity. There will be little critical response to Hick in these sections, for two reasons. First, astute readers will quickly

---

3. There are many technical details in all this that go beyond the scope of this book. By way of illustration, consider the statement, "If Nolan Ryan has struck out more batters than anyone else in baseball history, then Smoky Bear is a duck." There are two problems here: (1) No logical connection exists between the first and second clauses; and (2) while the first clause is true, the second is not. Even Hick admits that if the first clause (Jesus Christ is God) is true, then all the consequences that are so damaging to pluralism would also be true.

realize that Hick provides little or no argumentation for his positions. Second, Hick's claims depend on outdated New Testament scholarship. What Hick presents is often pure speculation or mere dogmatism.

In the last two sections we finally uncover Hick's putative reasons for his positions. One line of Hick's argument flows from certain claims he makes as to the historical unreliability of the New Testament documents. If what Christians think they know about Jesus is actually unsupported by trustworthy historical evidence, then many essential Christian beliefs about him — including the Incarnation — will suffer irreparable damage. Hick's second line of argument attacks the Christian belief that Jesus Christ possesses two natures (divine and human) in one person. The last part of the chapter reviews Hick's challenges to essential Christian beliefs about the person and work of Jesus Christ.

## THE INCARNATION AS MYTH

John Hick holds that the early Christian belief that Jesus Christ is God incarnate is a myth. By "myth" Hick means a story or image that is not literally true. But while myths are never literally true, they may be practically true. The practical truth becomes apparent when the myth is applied appropriately to some object or person.[4]

Hick develops a clever analogy in defense of his view of myth: He tells the story of a man in love who declares that his Helen is the sweetest and prettiest girl in the whole world. While such an exaggeration cannot be literally true, it may still be mythically true if it expresses an appropriate attitude of the lover toward the person he loves. In a similar way, early Christians took the simple expression "Jesus is my Lord and Savior," a psychological statement, and transformed it into a metaphysical claim: "Jesus is the *only* Lord and Savior." Hick wishes people would stop thinking of the Incarnation as a metaphysical "truth" and regard it as an "imaginative reconstruction" that expresses "the Christian's devotion to Jesus as the one

---

4. See Hick, "Jesus and the World Religions," 178.

who has made the heavenly Father real to him."[5] Jesus is not *the* Savior; he is only *my* savior, Hick contends.

Reducing the Incarnation to the status of myth sets up Hick's interpretation of the Atonement and the Resurrection. In Hick's view, no one is saved by Jesus. The nature of the Christian experience of forgiveness and reconciliation led naturally to thinking about Jesus' death as somehow connected with this forgiveness, and this led in turn to the idea of atonement. There is no special way in which Jesus is unique in the matter of salvation; God's salvation is available through other religions and other "saviors."

Hick also rejects any view that Jesus' alleged resurrection sets him apart from all other supposed "saviors" and provides a reason to believe in his deity.[6] Hick acknowledges the likelihood that the disciples of the Gospels had experiences of Jesus after his death. But Hick claims we do not know what this event was, nor does it really matter — the disciples never connected any "resurrection-event" with Christ's supposed deity. Not surprisingly, Hick ignores Romans 1:4: "who through the Spirit of holiness was declared with power to be the Son of God by his resurrection from the dead: Jesus Christ our Lord."

Whatever we make of the resurrection-event, Hick continues, all it shows is that Jesus "had a special place within God's providence; but this was not equivalent to seeing him as literally divine. For Jesus is not said to have risen in virtue of a divine nature he himself possessed but to have been raised by God."[7] So, for Hick, the bottom line in all this is that (1) he doubts that a physical resurrection really occurred, and (2) even if it did, it would not prove that Jesus is God.

## WHAT DID JESUS BELIEVE
## AND CLAIM ABOUT HIMSELF?

Hick denies that Jesus was either conscious of being God or claimed to be God. Hick's reasoning on this is that (1) Jesus was not and is not God, but (2) if he *thought* he was God, then Jesus

5. Hick, *God Has Many Names*, 125 – 26.
6. Hick, "Jesus and the World Religions," 170.
7. Ibid., 171.

was severely handicapped psychologically, and therefore, (3) if he claimed to be God and knew it was not so, then Jesus was morally deficient. Hick the pluralist has no interest in destroying the reputation of the man Jesus, only the supposedly divine Jesus. Hence the importance of trying to show that Jesus himself never believed he was God.[8]

Further, Hick states, although Jesus may have been conscious of a special calling from God, he was not conscious of being God.[9] He aways knew that he was just a human being.

> I see the Nazarene, then, as intensely and overwhelmingly conscious of the reality of God. He was a man of God, living in the unseen presence of God, and addressing God as *abba*, father. His spirit was open to God and his life a continuous response to the divine love as both utterly gracious and demanding. He was so powerfully God conscious that his life vibrated, as it were, to the divine life; and as a result his hands could heal the sick, and the "poor in spirit" were kindled to new life in his presence.... Thus in Jesus' presence, we should have felt that we are in the presence of God — not in the sense that the man Jesus literally *is* God, but in the sense that he was so totally conscious of God that we could catch something of that consciousness by spiritual contagion.[10]

There is nothing new, of course, in Hick's portrait of Jesus. Many unitarians have said the same things.

According to Hick, then, Jesus was simply a human being who managed to attain a special awareness of God and God's love:

> Now we want to say of Jesus that he was so vividly conscious of God as the loving heavenly Father, and so startlingly open to God and so fully his servant and instrument, that the divine love was expressed, and in that sense incarnated, in his life. This was not a matter (as it is in official Christian doctrine) of Jesus having two complete natures, one human and the other divine. He was wholly human; but whenever self-giving love in response to the love of God is lived out in a

---

8. See Hick, *God Has Many Names,* 28, 72 – 73, 125; and also Hick's "Jesus and the World Religions," 171 – 73.

9. John Hick, *God and the Universe of Faiths* (London: Macmillan, 1973), 163.

10. Hick, "Jesus and the World Religions," 172.

→ human life, to that extent the divine love has become incarnate on earth.[11]

Two points are worth making here. First, why should not the church's early response to Jesus, which Hick suggests resulted in an unwarranted apotheosis, be permitted as itself an authentic response to his persona? Does it not conform to Hick's own criterion?[12] Second, there is justification for thinking that Hick is toying with the word "incarnate," seeking to retain the term because of its historic significance but totally stripping it of its historic meaning.

All this leads to the conclusion that Jesus possessed no consciousness of his own deity. Rather, Jesus was so conscious of God's presence around and within him that he could not help but have a profound impact on those in his presence. Being in Jesus' presence produced an effect like being in God's presence.

## HOW THE CHURCH TURNED JESUS INTO GOD

Hick contends that through a long, gradual process the Christian church deified Jesus — a predictable testimony to the powerful psychological impact Jesus had on people. But this impact was not a result of Christ's actual deity; rather, it was a consequence of the powerful presence of God's love in Jesus' life. It was understandable that many would find it difficult to distinguish Jesus from the God whose presence they felt so powerfully when they were near the Teacher. These experiences of Jesus over time were part of the process that led eventually to a declaration of his deity at the Council of Nicea (A.D. 325).[13] A similar transformation over a long period of time occurred in the case of the title "Son of God." Hick repeats every liberal theory offered about this expression. Some cultures of the first century, he suggests, commonly thought some humans had been ele-

---

11. Hick, *God Has Many Names,* 58 – 59.

12. For an excellent source on the view that the attitude of the early church toward Jesus cannot be attributed to the objective contours of Jesus' ministry, see Royce Gruenler, *New Approaches to Jesus and the Gospels* (Grand Rapids: Baker, 1982). I am indebted to Douglas Geivett on this point.

13. See Hick, "Jesus and the World Religions," 173 – 74.

vated to the status of gods. At other times the prevailing culture supposedly contained examples of deity existing in human form. Both claims rest on a faulty understanding of the so-called mystery religions of the Hellenistic World.[14]

Hick's most common tactic is to cite the Old Testament application of the expression "Son of God" to King David (Ps. 2:7), which makes it a metaphor. The Old Testament supposedly established its metaphorical nature, and it is easy to see how the early church came to apply the same metaphor to Jesus, who was thought to be a descendent of David. But the original term carried no connotation of deity, Hick contends, so the early church may have thought of Jesus as a "Son of God" in a nonliteral, metaphorical sense. The damage was created when, over several centuries, the church slowly transposed "Son of God" to "God the Son." In fact, Hick believes that such a view is already apparent in the fourth gospel, which he regards as a late contribution to the New Testament.[15]

## ARE JESUS AND CHRISTIANITY UNIQUE?

Christians make the uniqueness of Christ a fundamental element of Christian belief. To call something unique is to affirm that it is the only one of its kind. To apply this line of thinking to Jesus is to declare that he is the one and only mediator between God and man, the one and only Savior. Not surprisingly, Hick disagrees. Hick and Paul Knitter begin their book *The Myth of Christian Uniqueness* by explaining that

> We are calling "Christian uniqueness" a "myth," not because we think that talk of the uniqueness of Christianity is purely and simply false, and so to be discarded. Rather, we feel that such talk, like all mythic language, must be understood carefully; it must be interpreted; its "truth" lies not on its literal

---

14. See Ronald Nash, *The Gospel and the Greeks* (Dallas: Probe Books, 1992), part 2. The sources for Hick's claims in this paragraph include his chapter, "Jesus and the World Religions," 175. See also John Hick, "The Non-Absoluteness of Christianity" in *The Myth of Christian Uniqueness*, ed. John Hick and Paul F. Knitter (Maryknoll, N.Y.: Orbis Books, 1987), 31.

15. See Hick, "Jesus and the World Religions," 175.

surface but within its ever-changing historical and personal meaning.[16]

These thinkers dislike the idea that "the uniqueness of Christianity" has assumed "a larger mythological meaning. It has come to signify the unique definitiveness, absoluteness, normativeness, superiority of Christianity in comparison with other religions of the world."[17] Hick and Knitter reject this sense of the term. The only way Christianity is unique for pluralists is the way any religion is unique: only one of its kind exists and nothing else is exactly like it. But this watered-down sense of uniqueness has nothing to do with absoluteness or superiority.

Hick handles the supposed uniqueness of Jesus in a similar way. While he views Jesus as the unique founder of Christianity, the claim is trivial, because when any religion has only one founder, that person is "unique" for that religion. But outside the bounds of Christian faith, there is nothing at all unique about Jesus. Other religions are equally acceptable paths to God. Hence, the founders of these other religions are as unique in their way as Jesus is in his. Jesus' uniqueness is relative, not absolute.

## THE DEPENDABILITY OF THE NEW TESTAMENT

I believe that Hick's claims as we have reviewed them here function more as examples of how pluralists hope to counter historic Christian thinking about Jesus with alternative ways of thinking. Before any of Hick's claims can command respect, it will be necessary — sooner or later — for him to go beyond making dogmatic assertions to forging real arguments. We have now come upon the first of those arguments: he attacks the documents that Christians use to ground their belief in a divine Christ.

Hick believes that attempts to speak informatively about Jesus on the basis of solid information encounter great confusion and uncertainty in the biblical sources. In his view, "New

---

16. Hick and Knitter, preface to *The Myth of Christian Uniqueness*, vii.
17. Ibid.

Testament scholarship has shown how fragmentary and ambiguous are the data available to us as we try to look back across nineteen and a half centuries, and at the same time how large and how variable is the contribution of the imagination to our 'pictures' of Jesus."[18]

### Hick's Historical Skepticism

Hick falls back on a number of old and outdated attacks on the reliability and integrity of the New Testament documents. He alleges that the data Christians appeal to are incomplete and indecisive as we look back over two millennia of history at the "largely unknown man of Nazareth."[19]

This adoption of historical criticism is understandable, given Hick's objectives. If he can present a halfway plausible case that the historical Jesus is unknown or even unknowable, perhaps he can make it appear that the Christian doctrines he dislikes can be separated from any foundation in historical truth. Yet he is surprisingly silent about the New Testament scholars whom he enlists in support of his skepticism about the historical Jesus. Our not knowing exactly whom he has in mind makes any evaluation of his claim rather difficult. If Hick really were knowledgeable about New Testament scholarship, he would probably be less dogmatic on the subject, for serious biblical scholars are deeply divided on the issues that promote his skepticism. It would appear, however, that he has in view either proponents of the form-critical approach to the New Testament or proponents of the method known as redaction-criticism.  While both schools of thought have fueled skepticism about the historical Jesus, they both also have tended to fade from center stage. This fact certainly makes it appear as though Hick's position is based on outdated scholarship. Even more ironic is the fact that neither of these two methodologies entails Hick's kind of skepticism apart from considerable reliance on questionable presuppositions.

---

18. Hick, "Jesus and the World Religions," 167.
19. Ibid., 177–78.

## Form-Criticism

Proponents of form-criticism viewed the Gospels as the products of a long and complex process by which an original collection of oral traditions about Jesus came to be preserved because of their practical relevance for the church at a time some distance removed from eyewitness testimony. Form-critics emphasized the role of the Gospels as interpretations of Jesus' life and teaching. They deemphasized any search for objective, dispassionate, eyewitness reports of what the church believed about Jesus at the time the events supposedly occurred. The extent to which the Gospels were reliable sources of information about the historical Jesus became a question to which form-critics gave different, often conflicting answers.

While "New Testament scholarship" — a term Hick uses repeatedly — has moved well beyond form-criticism, the method had some positive value. As a neutral method, it helped produce some valuable insights.[20] Its more debatable side became apparent when the neutral method became mixed with negative, destructive presuppositions. The historical skepticism that Hick may have picked up from some form-critics was not a conclusion mandated by the method but a presupposition linked to the method by theological liberals already inclined toward such a view.

By itself, form-criticism does not oblige anyone to conclude that the early church invented its stories about Jesus. The method has been adopted by people who believe the stories were accurate recollections of what Jesus did and said and so were preserved because of their relevance for some later life-situation in the church. Historian A. N. Sherwin-White comments, "It is astonishing that while Graeco-Roman historians have been growing in confidence, the twentieth-century study of the Gospel narratives, starting from no less promising material, has taken so gloomy a turn in the development of form-criticism that the more advanced exponents of it apparently maintain . . .

---

20. See Ronald Nash, *Christian Faith and Historical Understanding* (Dallas: Probe Books, 1984), 64–72.

that the historical Christ is unknowable and the history of his mission cannot be written."[21]

The real problem in all this is not with form-criticism *per se*, but with the undefended assumption that the Gospels witness primarily to the life-situation of the church at some later stage of its history and only secondarily to the historical Jesus. But surely it is consistent with the form-critical method to recognize both the role that a later life-situation might have had in preserving a tradition and the reality of the historical events to which the tradition points.

Instead of assuming that the early church fabricated stories about Jesus to help it deal with its problems, it makes better sense to assume that practical relevance led the church to preserve statements originally made by Jesus. D. M. Baillie, for one, complains that it seldom seemed to occur to some form-critics "that the story may have been handed on simply or primarily because it was *true*, because the incident had actually taken place in the ministry of Jesus, and was therefore of great interest to his followers, even if they sometimes failed to understand it."[22]

It is one thing to note that the Gospel writers selected from the material available to them and applied it to practical uses. It is quite another to suggest that they felt no constraints against inventing new traditions if doing so suited some practical purpose. Selectivity does not entail creativity

A pivotal issue in the debate is where to place the burden of proof. Skeptics argue that the burden of proof rests on those who regard the biblical sources as authentic. But why should it not be the skeptic who has the burden of proof? Why not presume that if anything is to be proved, it must be the *inauthenticity* of Jesus' sayings? I could go on in regard to this widely repudiated theory,[23] but it should be obvious that the assured results of "New Testament scholarship" of this kind provides extremely weak grounds for Hick's historical skepticism. But

21. A. N. Sherwin-White, *Roman Society and Roman Life in the New Testament* (New York: Oxford University Press, 1963), 187.

22. D. M. Baillie, *God Was in Christ* (New York: Scribner's, 1948), 57.

23. For more on this topic, see Nash, *Christian Faith and Historical Understanding*, chap. 4.

perhaps he draws his skepticism from the second school we have mentioned, redaction-criticism.

### Redaction-Criticism

While form-critics concentrated on smaller independent units of material within the Gospels, redaction-critics were more interested in the Gospels as literary wholes. They viewed the Gospel writers as more than mere compilers and arrangers; rather, they were theologians whose arrangement of material was affected by their theological interests and their intentions.

But why should this lead us to assume that the Gospel writers *invented* any of their material? It need not. Although it is easy to identify theological interests at work in the Gospels, it requires a whole set of additional presuppositions to conclude that the Evangelists produced only imaginative interpretations of Jesus with loose or even nonexistent historical ties.

As with form-criticism, a detailed account of redaction-criticism would take us far afield from the study at hand. Our discussion should make it clear that form-criticism and redaction-criticism are not necessarily incompatible with either a high view of Scripture or the conviction that the New Testament picture of Jesus is grounded on trustworthy historical data. Hick's appeal to "New Testament scholarship" — as though this single expression somehow legitimizes one of his basic claims against New Testament Christology — does more than paper over his begging the question. It also shows how inadequate Hick's grasp of New Testament scholarship really is, a fact that will become even more evident as we continue the discussion about Christology.

### "Behold How Much the Skeptic Knoweth"

There is an ironic twist in the way Hick builds his case for skepticism about the Jesus of history. If we take Hick at his word, the New Testament is profoundly unreliable as a source of historical information about Jesus. But it is important to link this skepticism with all that Hick himself claims to *know* about the historical Jesus.

Early in 1993, R. Douglas Geivett attended a lecture given by Hick in Indianapolis. Hick pointed to Jesus as a powerful example of a person who holds Hick's own view of salvation. It occurred to Geivett that "Hick's moderately high view of Jesus as a paradigmatic saint depends upon our having reliable historical data. In other words, the authentic Jesus must be discernible in the Gospel record if Hick is entitled to regard him with the kind of respect he does."[24]

Geivett recognized that someone should ask Hick about his criterion for selecting which biblical data are authentic and which are not. His exchange with Hick proves to be quite illuminating.

Geivett observed that the biblical record shows Jesus saying and doing things that many people would regard as incompatible with Hick's allegedly saintly Jesus. Hick asked for an example or two. As Geivett relates it,

> I referred to places where it is alleged that Jesus drove the money-changers from the temple with a whip and confronted the hypocrisy of the religious leaders of his day in very strong terms (calling them "whitewashed tombs"). Hick's reply was twofold. First, he said he was prepared to identify these reports as gradual additions to the tradition. Second, he indicated that if Jesus really did act in the way described in these instances, then "he was appallingly anti-Semitic."[25]

It appears that Hick suffers from a blind spot or two. As Geivett observes, "Clearly, Hick's own moral intuitions have become a control on what he is willing to acknowledge as an authentic account of what Jesus said and did. Never mind the historical and manuscript evidence, and the difficulty of picking and choosing among pericopes."[26] And never mind about consistency within Hick's own system of thought! It appears that Hick's only criterion for distinguishing between authentic and inauthentic biblical material is compatibility with his own position.

---

24. R. Douglas Geivett in a personal letter, April 5, 1993. Used by permission.
25. Ibid.
26. Ibid.

## Hick's Claims About the Evolution of Early Christian Belief

Hick contends that the church's understanding of Jesus evolved from an early commitment to him as a powerful person in whom they sensed the presence of God into increasingly complex theological constructions about Jesus as Son of God, then as God the Son, and finally as the Second Person of the Trinity. Although these kinds of claims were popular decades ago, scholars have more recently declared such theories untenable.[27]

First, British scholar C. F. D. Moule has found some weaknesses in Hick's views, especially in the claim that neither Jesus nor his early followers regarded him as divine. Moule disputes Hick's idea — that the evolutionary course of Christology borrowed significantly from beliefs outside of Christianity — as being inconsistent with the New Testament. Moule argues instead that the early Christian recognition of Jesus as divine reflected a pattern in which "the various estimates of Jesus reflected in the New Testament [are], in essence, only attempts to describe what was already there from the beginning. They are not successive additions of something new, but only the drawing out and articulating of what is there."[28] From the very start, Moule insists, Jesus was someone who could be appropriately described in the very ways he came to be described during the years in which the New Testament was written, that is, as "Lord" and "God."[29]

Second, German New Testament scholar Martin Hengel provides evidence for the claim that the early church called Jesus the "Son of God" during the years between A.D. 30 and 50.[30]

---

27. For examples, see F. F. Bruce, The *New Testament Documents: Are They Reliable?* 5th ed. (Grand Rapids: Eerdmans, 1982); Oscar Cullmann, *The Christology of the New Testament*, rev. ed., trans. Shirley C. Guthrie and Charles A. M. Hall (Philadelphia: Westminster, 1963); Joachim Jeremias, *New Testament Theology*, trans. John Bowden (New York: Scribner's, 1971); C. F. D. Moule, *The Phenomenon of the New Testament* (London: SCM Press, 1967); and Craig Blomberg, *The Historical Reliability of the Gospels* (Downers Grove, Ill.: InterVarsity Press, 1987).

28. C. F. D. Moule, *The Origin of Christology* (Cambridge: Cambridge University Press, 1977), 2 – 3.

29. Ibid., 4.

30. Martin Hengel, *The Son of God: The Origin of Christology and the History of Jewish-Hellenistic Religion* (Philadelphia: Fortress, 1976), 2, 10.

It seems clear that Hick will have to present a much stronger case than he has set forth so far if he hopes to persuade evangelicals that the deity of Christ is a metaphysical theory constructed late in the first century.[31]

*1 cor 15 creed*

### The Positive Evidence That Hick Ignores

Sir Norman Anderson faults Hick for greatly exaggerating "the paucity of positive evidence we have about the one to whom he refers as the 'largely unknown man of Nazareth.'"[32] Hick ignores Jesus' own statements about his coming death, as attested by the Synoptic writers (Matt. 20:17 – 19; 26:12f.; Mark 10:33f.; Luke 18:31 – 34). He ignores Jesus' act of forgiving sins, an act in which Jesus acted as God (Mark 2:8 – 12). When Jesus forgave people, he went beyond what any mere human is able to do. Any of us can forgive people for the things they do to *us*. Jesus did that, of course; but he also forgave people for the sins they had committed against others! In all these cases, Jesus acted as though the sins against other humans were violations of *his* holy law and thus sins against him as well.

Paul's earliest letters, usually dated to about two decades after the Resurrection, reveal the existence of a developed Christology. This shows that the high view of Christ to which Hick objects can be found in documents that many scholars consider the earliest of all New Testament writings.[33] In 2 Corinthians 13:14 Paul affirms Jesus' standing as God (as part of the Trinity). In Philippians 2:5 – 11 he claims Jesus' equality with God. In 1 Thessalonians 1:10 he presents Jesus as God's only medium of deliverance. It is impossible to explain away such statements as late-first-century theorizing.

Nor should anyone overlook the contradictions in Hick's position, a point already noted. After asserting his skepticism about the historical Jesus, Hick fills his writings with numerous claims about how this largely unknown Jesus still manages to

---

31. See Michael Green, "Jesus in the New Testament," in *The Truth of God Incarnate*, ed. Michael Green (London: Hodder & Stoughton, 1977), 20.

32. Sir Norman Anderson, *The Mystery of Incarnation* (London: Hodder & Stoughton, 1978), 64.

33. Moule, *The Origin of Christology*, 6 – 7.

disclose God's presence and love. Hick amazes us with all that *he* knows about the "unknown Nazarene."

### Hick and the Fourth Gospel

Hick's dislike for the fourth gospel is understandable, given its strong and unequivocal support for the deity of Christ (John 10:30; 14:6, 9). If Jesus really said the things attributed to him in the fourth gospel, Hick's efforts to attack the high Christology that grounds exclusivism would be doomed. According to Hick, Christology must not and cannot be based on the supposition that the historical Jesus really said what John's gospel attributes to him.

But Hick's claim that the fourth gospel rewrites Jesus' teaching is groundless. As C. F. D. Moule has shown, a supernatural Christology is clearly present in the Synoptic Gospels.[34] Even if Hick could get rid of the fourth gospel, his problems would remain.

All this shows the extent to which Hick's attack on the church's Christology depends on his question-begging appeal to certain unnamed New Testament scholars whose positions are at the very least contradicted by scholars of equal reputation. But Hick ignores any New Testament authority who disagrees with his prejudices. Anyone consulting the New Testament scholars cited in my notes will quickly discover how badly outdated both Hick and his authorities are. The rest of his assertions noted earlier in this chapter are pure speculation and exercises in liberal dogmatism with no credibility.[35]

## HICK'S ATTACK ON THE TWO NATURES OF CHRIST

One final issue must be examined, even though it will entail a long and somewhat technical discussion. That issue is Hick's attack on the doctrine of Christ's two natures, human and divine.

---

34. Ibid., 6.

35. For other critiques of positions similar to Hick's, see R. N. Longenecker, *The Christology of Early Jewish Christianity* (London: SCM, 1970); I. Howard Marshall, *The Origins of New Testament Christology* (Downers Grove, Ill.: InterVarsity Press, 1976); and H. H. Rowden, *Christ the Lord* (Leicester, England: Inter-Varsity Press, 1982).

Christians use the word *Incarnation* to express their belief that the birth of Jesus Christ marked the entrance of the eternal and divine Son of God into the human race. The Incarnation is an essential Christian belief. If this doctrine is false, the Christian faith is false. Correct thinking about Jesus Christ diminishes neither his full and complete humanity nor his full and complete deity. Jesus Christ is God — let there be no mistake about this. But he is also human. Any wavering on either claim results in a defective Christology and a heretical faith.

We are not surprised, then, when opponents of the historic Christian faith take aim at this core doctrine. The Incarnation is an inviting target, not only because it is a central belief, but also because it seems susceptible to the charge that this is one point where Christians believe a logical contradiction. Hick echoes this charge when he states that claims that Jesus is both God and man are as self-contradictory and meaningless as statements that a drawn figure is a square circle.[36] To him, the doctrine of Christ's two natures is clearly a logical contradiction and hence necessarily false.

The general line of Hick's thought goes as follows: The Christian God has attributes such as omnipotence, omniscience, incorporeality, and sinlessness. God also exists necessarily, which means, among other things, that there can be neither beginning nor end to his existence. Moreover, these properties belong to God essentially or necessarily, which is to say that if God were to lose any of these essential properties, he would cease to be God. A being cannot be God if he lacks omnipotence, omniscience, and the like.

But when we reflect on the nature of humanness, we encounter creatures with precisely the opposite properties. Human beings are *not* omnipotent, omniscient, incorporeal, or sinless. Nor do we exist necessarily. Our existence is contingent — that is, dependent on many things other than ourselves. Given these seemingly obvious incompatibilities between God and man, how could any being possibly be both God and man?

This is a serious difficulty. Developing an appropriate response to Hick's challenge will require hard thinking about

---

36. Hick, "Jesus and the World Religions," 178.

complex issues. Thomas Morris, a philosophy professor at Notre Dame, has sought a solution to the problem that leaves the two-natures doctrine intact.[37] Morris's argument has two parts. First, he attempts to show that the two-natures doctrine does not entail a logical contradiction. Second, he presents a theory that he hopes will make the doctrine easier to understand.

Some scholars question the second part of Morris's argument as verging on an ancient heresy known as Nestorianism.[38] Because of these reservations, I will not deal with that second argument in this book.

The fact is, if Morris succeeds in the first part, it does not matter what happens in the second. A successful defense of the two-natures doctrine from the charge of logical inconsistency will stand on its own. It is one thing for a doctrine about the eternal God to surpass human understanding (Rom. 11:33 – 35; Job 11:7 – 8; Isa. 55:8 – 9); it is quite another for that belief to lack logical coherence. Just because something is above reason, it does not follow that it is against reason. Morris's defense of the logical coherence of the two-natures doctrine succeeds even if his more ambitious attempt to explain the doctrine may not.

According to Morris, we can work our way out of the logical problem if we first understand and then properly apply three philosophical distinctions, namely,

1. The distinction between essential and nonessential properties;

2. The distinction between essential and common properties; and

3. The distinction between being *fully* human and *merely* human.

---

37. Morris's argument appears in both a book, *The Logic of God Incarnate* (Ithaca, N.Y.: Cornell University Press, 1986), and a more popular article, "Understanding God Incarnate," *Asbury Theological Journal* 43 (1988): 63 – 77.

38. Nestorius was a fifth-century Patriarch of Constantinople. Since none of his writings survive, our knowledge of his supposed heresy depends entirely on discussions by his opponents and therefore the debate is one of the more obscure in the history of Christian doctrine. Hence, it is entirely possible that Morris is not a Nestorian, just as it is possible that Nestorius was not one either. Morris seemingly approaches Nestorianism because he suggests that the person of Jesus Christ possesses two overlapping minds, a finite human mind encompassed in an omniscient divine mind.

### Essential and Nonessential Properties

A property is a feature or characteristic of something. We can identify many of the properties of Socrates simply by filling in the blank in the following sentence: "Socrates is _____." All these terms denote properties or traits of Socrates: "bald," "citizen of Athens," "honorable," "short," "the husband of Xanthippe." Everything has properties, and one way we refer to those properties is by using them as predicates applied to a given subject.

Next, we must recognize that properties come in two types, essential and nonessential. Consider a red ball. The color of the object is nonessential in the sense that if we somehow changed the color to yellow or green, the object would still be a ball. But with a ball, the property of roundness is an essential property. We cannot have a ball that is not round.[39] If we change this feature of our object, it is no longer a ball.

Put in its simplest terms, an essential property is one that cannot be changed or lost without the object in question ceasing to be the *kind* of thing it is. Roundness is an essential property of being a ball. When an object that once was a member of the class of all balls loses its roundness, it also loses its membership in that class.

A number of properties are essential to the being of God, including at least the following: necessary existence, omnipotence, omniscience, and sinlessness. Any being lacking these and the other essential properties of deity could *not* be God. Obviously, then, when Christians affirm that Jesus is God, they are also affirming that Jesus possesses eternally and necessarily all the essential properties of God. That much is easy.

Matters become more difficult when we try to identify the essential properties of a human being. Aristotle thought that

---

39. A friend of mine in Plano, Texas, expresses doubts about my point and notes that a football, while called a ball, is certainly not round. Since my purpose is to help readers to grasp the nature of an essential property, her objection shows that my example has been successful to that degree. But what shall I say about that inflated ellipsoid made of pigskin that we call a football? Perhaps we call it a ball because it is close enough to a real ball to show us how analogies work. Or perhaps I should identify some property other than roundness as the essential property common to baseballs, basketballs, and footballs.

rationality (thinking and reasoning) was an essential property of humans. Rationality certainly seems to be one property among others that make up the essence of a human being, that set humans apart from other creatures on our planet.

In his criticism of the Incarnation, Hick makes a crucial error in believing that such properties as *lacking omnipotence, lacking omniscience,* and *lacking sinlessness* are also essential in some way to humanness. But to proceed further with our argument we must first introduce the distinction between essential properties and common properties.

### Essential Properties and Common Properties

What Morris calls common properties are often mistaken for essential properties. This error is the basis for believing that the doctrine of the Incarnation entails a contradiction. A common property is any property that human beings typically possess without also being essential. Morris gives the example of having ten fingers. Because almost every human has ten fingers, it is a common human property. But clearly, having ten fingers is not essential to being a human being. A person can lose one or more fingers and still be a human being. Therefore the common human property of having ten fingers is not an essential property.

Likewise, we could say that living on earth is a common human property. But it is conceivable that at some time in the future, some people will be born and live out their entire lives on other planets. So once again, a property that we have found common to all people turns out not to be essential.

Now, we could say that all of us — each human being apart from Jesus — are characterized by properties that are the counterparts of such divine properties as omnipotence and omniscience. But on what basis can we say that these limitations are somehow essential to our humanness? These limitations are possibly only common human properties, not essential ones.

### Being Fully *Human* and Being Merely *Human*

Morris explains that "An individual is fully human [in any case where] that individual has all essential human properties, all the properties composing basic human nature. An individual is *merely human* if he has all those properties *plus* some additional limitation properties as well, properties such as that of lacking omnipotence, that of lacking omniscience, and so on."[40]

Orthodox Christians, Morris adds, insist on the claim that "Jesus was fully human without being merely human."[41] This means two things: (1) Jesus possessed *all* the properties that are essential to being a human being, and (2) Jesus also possessed all the properties that are essential to deity. Morris suggests that the properties Hick makes so much of and insists are essential to humanity (such as lacking omniscience) are simply being confused with common properties.

Once Christians understand these distinctions about properties they are equipped to counter challenges such as those of John Hick that orthodox Christology is self-contradictory. The orthodox understanding of the Incarnation expresses the claims that (1) Jesus Christ is fully God — that is, he possesses all the essential properties of God, (2) Jesus Christ is also fully human — that is, he possesses all the essential properties of a human being, none of which turn out to be limiting properties, and (3) Jesus Christ was not merely human — that is, he did not possess any of the limiting properties that are in fact complements of the divine attributes. In the face of these distinctions, the contradiction Hick is concerned about disappears.

### Hick's Response to Morris

John Hick apparently saw the strength in Morris's rebuttal to the charge that the doctrine of the Incarnation is logically incoherent and responded to it in 1989 in a very long review article.[42] Just as Morris's argument had two parts, so Hick's response has two distinct sections. It is noteworthy that almost eighty percent of Hick's article deals with Morris's less than satisfactory efforts to explain the Incarnation. But many Christians themselves are not interested in defending this second part of Morris's argument because of its tendencies toward Nestorianism.

---

40. Morris, "Understanding God Incarnate," 66.
41. Ibid.
42. John Hick, "The Logic of God Incarnate," *Religious Studies* 24 (1989): 409–23.

What is ironic about Hick's long critique of Morris's second argument is the way it mirrors ancient *orthodox* attacks on Nestorianism. This leaves us with a situation in which Hick echoes the thinking of ancient orthodox Christians but mistakenly believes these arguments advance his attack on the Incarnation. Therefore a traditional or conservative Christian could readily agree with the last eleven pages of Hick's article without accepting Hick's conclusion.[43] But no matter how instructive and interesting that discussion may be, it seems to be irrelevant to the claim that the two-natures doctrine is logically inconsistent.

So this leaves us with Hick's four-page treatment of the first part of Morris's argument. But what Hick regards as a refutation of Morris is hardly a model of clarity or persuasiveness. It is at best an attempt to "muddy the waters." Hick does this by trying to counter Morris's distinctions (such as that between common and essential properties) with some puzzling examples (such as being fully human and being fully an alligator). This avails little since Hick himself admits that Morris can escape his challenge in a variety of ways[44] — which leaves us wondering why Hick goes to the trouble. We are left with a two-part reply to Morris in which part one is by Hick's own admission inconclusive and in which part two is irrelevant.

Christians can safely conclude, then, that even though they cannot understand everything about the Incarnation and the relationship between Christ's human and divine natures, the doctrines are logically coherent and Hick's attempted rebuttal fails.

## SUMMARY

Hick's initial thunder and lightning about the Incarnation turn out to be no more than a series of dogmatic assertions.

---

43. I must add two qualifications to this sentence. First, Hick suggests that because Morris fails adequately to explain the Incarnation, there is therefore no intelligible and acceptable way to do this. But clearly, the inability of humans to understand something now neither entails its falsity nor precludes their understanding it in the future. Second, Hick confuses Morris's Nestorian-like position with that of the Chalcedonian Council (A.D. 451), when in fact the church of the fifth century rejected Nestorius's views precisely because they appeared to conflict with the Chalcedonian formulation of the two-natures doctrine.

44. Hick, "The Logic of God Incarnate," 412.

Separated from any relevant arguments that function as a ground for his claims, they reveal much about Hick's present state of thinking but mount no serious challenge to the Christology of the orthodox church.

This is not the case with Hick's two major arguments, namely, his skepticism about the historical dependability of the New Testament and his allegation that the Incarnation involves Christians in a logically contradictory theory. My response to the first argument is that Hick relies on outdated critical theories and doubtful sources to make his case; my response to the second argument is that his failure to make adequate distinctions about the properties of humanness dooms his charge that the Incarnation is a self-contradictory and logically incoherent doctrine. I conclude that Hick's assault on the historical and orthodox Christian understanding of Jesus Christ fails.

Chapter Six

# FINAL THOUGHTS
# ON HICK'S PLURALISM

Several issues, most of them related to other pluralist criticisms of exclusivism, remain to be considered in part 1.

## THE ISSUE OF INTOLERANCE

The first of these issues is the frequently made accusation that exclusivism is immoral. W. C. Smith makes precisely this charge when he writes, "Exclusivism strikes more and more Christians as immoral."[1] Joseph Runzo accuses exclusivism of being "neither tolerable nor any longer intellectually honest in the context of our contemporary knowledge of others' faiths."[2]

The point here seems to be that Christian exclusivists are implicitly guilty of intolerance for holding that religious beliefs that are logically incompatible with what they believe must be false. In the presence of such intolerance, any number of other moral failings presumably become evident, including elitism, arrogance, spiritual pride, imperialism, triumphalism, and arbitrariness. John Hick accuses Christian exclusivists of "validating centuries of anti-Semitism, the colonial exploitation by Christian Europe of

---

1. Wilfred Cantrell Smith, "An Attempt at Summation," in *Christ's Lordship and Religious Pluralism,* ed. G. H. Anderson and T. F. Stransky (Maryknoll, N.Y.: Orbis Books, 1981), 202.
2. Joseph Runzo, "God, Commitment and Other Faiths: Pluralism vs. Relativism," *Faith and Philosophy* 5 (1988): 357.

what today we call the third world, and the subordination of women within a strongly patriarchal religious system."[3] This kind of name-calling is strictly out of order, however, because nowhere in any of his writings does Hick even come close to proving a causal connection between exclusivism and the events he mentions.

It is always easier to persuade people to dissociate themselves from positions that are made to look ludicrous or mean. While I have met a few exclusivists who exhibited moral failings like those mentioned, I have no reason to think that these attitudes were a direct consequence of their exclusivism. Many people are mean and nasty in expressing their ideas, including some nonexclusivists. That I do not believe all the things you believe hardly makes me guilty of intolerance, imperialism, egotism, arbitrariness, or oppression.

If dissenting entails an explicit or implicit condemnation of certain beliefs, then by implication the dissenter displays the attitude and conviction that his or her beliefs are superior to mine. Now, Hick himself dissents from the beliefs held by exclusivists. So the criticism cuts both ways; Hick falls prey to the same moral failings he attributes to exclusivists.

Some people hold that any difference of opinion implies rejection of the person. Paul Griffiths and Delmas Lewis suggest that pluralists seem "to believe that you can only be nice to people if you agree with them. This seems clearly false. It is both logically and practically possible for us, as Christians, to respect and revere worthy representatives of other traditions while still believing — on rational grounds — that some aspects of their world-view are simply mistaken."[4] Person A might like, respect, and trust person B even though B believes a clearly false proposition such as "The world is flat." So it is clear that "We can disagree with people and still be nice to them, even if historically we have not always done so."[5]

---

3. John Hick, *Disputed Questions in Theology and Philosophy* (New Haven: Yale University Press, 1993), viii.

4. Paul Griffiths and Delmas Lewis, "On Grading Religions, Seeing Truth, and Being Nice to People — a Reply to Professor Hick," *Religious Studies* 19 (1983): 77.

5. Ibid.

Philosopher Steve Davis argues:

> All peoples, including evangelicals, wish for a harmonious world religious community; global cooperation, mutual understanding, and trust are indeed badly needed. But what says that such a community can be achieved only on the basis of agreement? One might have thought that something like the reverse is true. The only way in which people of various religions and cultures can come to understand and cooperate with one another is to honestly recognize their differences. Minimizing them or subsuming them under some unifying theory is not the way to proceed.[6]

It is helpful to distinguish between two kinds of tolerance. Moral tolerance is total acceptance of the other person as a human being who has a right to be treated with dignity and respect, even though he or she holds beliefs quite different from mine. The opposite of this, of course, is moral intolerance. All sorts of people may be guilty of moral intolerance; some may be exclusivists, but there is no necessary link between the two.

A different kind of tolerance appears when I am forbidden to judge or criticize the beliefs of anyone who disagrees with me. This second, unlabeled kind of tolerance insists that it is wrong, always and everywhere, to disagree with anyone who disagrees with me. Although some may choose to treat this position as a form of tolerance, thereby endowing it with an aura of saintliness, it is in fact a type of intellectual suicide. While Hick advances his cause by confusing these two kinds of tolerance and intolerance, he himself does not hesitate to disagree with anyone who disagrees with his pluralism. Yet it is the second type of intolerance — the kind that Hick himself practices — that is part and parcel of the moral attacks Hick and other pluralists make on exclusivists.

What about attempts to convert non-Christians to Christianity — is not that a display of intolerance? While evangelizing and proselytizing are sometimes carried out in an unworthy manner, I fail to see how any respectful attempt to

---

6. Steve Davis, "Evangelicals and the Religions of the World," *Reformed Journal* (June 1981): 10.

persuade another person to change his or her beliefs can be an instance of intolerance.

Nor does exclusivism obligate Christians to believe that everything taught by a non-Christian religion must be false. Christian exclusivists can recognize truthful concepts in other religions as well as valuable psychological and moral insights. Exclusivism need not entail narrow-mindedness, arrogance, insensitivity, or self-righteousness. R. Douglas Geivett explains, "It is of course appropriate to be charitable towards those who stand within different religious traditions. But a charitable response does not require a pluralist conclusion; it may even be opposed to a pluralist outlook. For charity will, it seems to me, take seriously and at face value the specific truth-claims embodied in the varied religious traditions. Christian [exclusivists], among others, are not likely to think of Hick's attitude toward them as particularly charitable."[7]

Upon closer examination, the moral attack on exclusivism appears shallow, unsound, hypocritical, and peevish and should be turned back upon the people who raise it. To assault people in such a personal way without justification is itself a moral failing; it is certainly more serious than wrongly accusing someone of defending a weak argument.

## GEOGRAPHIC AND CULTURAL CONDITIONING

In chapter 2 we noted in passing that one of Hick's earliest grounds for rejecting exclusivism is its alleged indifference to what he regards as the inescapable role of geographic and cultural conditioning in determining religious beliefs. People born in New Delhi, India, can hardly be blamed for becoming Hindus any more than someone born in Cisco, Texas, can be faulted for becoming a Baptist. If any of us had been born in Japan or China, Hick contends, it is unlikely that we would have become Christians.

---

7. R. Douglas Geivett, "John Hick's Approach to Religious Pluralism," *Proceedings of the Wheaton College Theology Conference* (1993), vol. 1, *The Challenge of Religious Pluralism: An Evangelical Analysis and Response*, 50.

There is obviously some truth to this observation. But how this observation is relevant to adjudging the truth or falsity of the Christian faith is unclear. Consider some of the dubious implications of Hick's position. For Hick, truth is a function of geography, that is, where people happen to have been born. This idea, carried to its logical implications, would make Nazism, cannibalism, infanticide, and witchcraft true because they could all be a result of geographic and cultural conditioning. And Hick's position also implies that beliefs can be true and false at the same time, true for people conditioned in one way and false for others. Furthermore, it implies that the truth of pluralism is also a function of geographic and cultural conditioning.

Still further, Roger Trigg notes, "Hick's argument, so far from encouraging us to give equal respect to all world religions, makes us wonder whether religion is any more valid than atheism,"[8] which also would be a function of geographic and cultural conditioning. Trigg finds it ironic that when Hick uses this appeal to encourage greater agreement between Christians and non-Christians, he "can only proceed by emptying the claims of either or both, of all real content."[9]

The biggest dilemma for Hick's contentions, however, is that he himself, born under cultural conditions that might be expected to produce a Christian, was converted to his present non-Christian, quasi-Eastern religious variety of pluralism. So Hick demonstrates again the irrelevancy and weakness of his arguments.

## EXCLUSIVISM, PLURALISM, AND THE LOVE OF "GOD"

We need to say something further about Hick's argument, raised in chapter 2, that Christian exclusivism is inconsistent with any adequate notion of divine love. Hick has specifically in mind the Christian doctrine of hell: surely an all-loving God

---

8. Roger Trigg, "Religion and the Threat of Relativism," *Religious Studies* 19 (1983): 298.
9. Ibid.

would save non-Christians or at least give them all an opportunity for salvation.

A more detailed treatment of this argument appears in part 2 as a response to similar charges from Christian inclusivists, but the point should not pass without comment here. As noted earlier, it is difficult to see how this argument fits with Hick's commitment to religious skepticism. We have observed that Hick feels strongly that God is unknown and unknowable. God is so unknowable, in fact, that the divine being should not even be called "God" any more. To abandon this skepticism would create serious problems for Hick's whole system of thought. So if Hick, the religious skeptic par excellence, insists on raising this charge, he can only do so on pain of contradicting himself.

But perhaps Hick's argument is hypothetical. Perhaps he intends to say that because Christians insist that God is love, their belief in divine love is incompatible with their horrible assertions of eternal judgment. Fair enough, but then we Christians must also point out that the Scriptures and Christian doctrine clearly teach that God has attributes other than love. He is also holy, an attribute that points to both the unqualified purity of his nature and also his holy hatred of sin. God's holy hatred of sin is analogous to the hatred a mother feels upon seeing a poisonous serpent about to strike a young child. Never once in his pluralist writings do I recall John Hick's mentioning the holiness of God. And the reason should be obvious: Universalists have no place in their theology for divine holiness.

The love of God that is such a matter of sentimental reverence for universalists is actually a holy love.[10] It is a love that will not and cannot ignore human sin — hence the cross of Christ (John 3:16). Nor can God's attributes be treated adequately without reference to God's holy justice. The major question that concerns Paul in his letter to the Romans is, "How can God be just and be the justifier of sinful men and women?" In universalist and pluralist systems, this question has absolutely no standing. But it is a fundamental matter of Christian belief. A

---

10. Notice how this analysis of even Hick's hypothetical argument inevitably returns to the question of whether he believes in divine love. As we have seen, Hick cannot; at least he cannot if he wishes to avoid contradicting his skepticism. And the moment he abandons his skepticism, his pluralism becomes untenable.

God who possesses the attributes of holy love and holy justice cannot pretend that sinners have not sinned. The punishment for sin is death. And so either sinners are punished for their own sins or else God takes their punishment upon himself. This truth is the heart of Christian belief and not the universalist-pluralist's sentimentalist account of "love."

## HICK AND ESCHATOLOGICAL VERIFICATION

Hick introduced the term "eschatological verification" some forty years ago as part of his efforts to defend the Christian faith from the intellectual threat of Logical Positivism.[11] This movement lost credibility for reasons that had nothing to do with Hick's theory, but the attention he received is no doubt one reason that he has been loathe to abandon the concept even though it now creates some difficulties for his pluralism and even though he also would like people to forget that he once had a moderate interest in defending Christianity.

A full treatment of eschatological verification in relation to Logical Positivism is not necessary here. The most relevant issue is that Logical Positivists thought while science could verify its claims through experience and experiments, Christianity was discredited because it could not. For example, a scientist claiming that litmus paper immersed in acid would change its color could "prove" both the truth and meaningfulness of his assertion by producing the results of a test. Take a piece of litmus paper, dip it in acid, and observe.

But consider a Christian claim such as "God exists." What kinds of empirical testing procedure can the Christian perform to "prove" that God exists? Because Christians cannot verify their basic claims, the Logical Positivists argued, these claims are meaningless; they are neither true nor false.

Hick took all this too seriously, as it turns out. Instead of mounting a more powerful attack against Logical Positivism, he argued that Christians can meet the verification challenge:

---

11. With Logical Positivism, a movement of the early twentieth century, the study of meaning became inextricably linked with linguistic philosophy, that is, philosophy entails a logical analysis of language. See Ronald Nash, *The Concept of God* (Grand Rapids: Zondervan, 1983), chap. 9.

Christianity can point to confirming experiences that will prove the truth and meaningfulness of its central claims. But there was a catch. The experiences that will finally prove whether Christianity's claims are true or false, cognitive or meaningless, will occur after each person's physical death; hence the term "eschatological verification." Hick has never repudiated this theory.

The relevance of Hick's position on this issue to his more recent views should be obvious. Some day we all will finally discover whether this or that religion, whether this or that theory about religion, is true or not. Hick cannot rule out the possibility that after death, during the process of eschatological verification, one religion will turn out to be true after all and one definitive concept of God will prove correct. In fact, Hick could not rule out this possibility even if he decided today to repudiate his theory of eschatological verification.

This raises a serious problem for anyone tempted to become a pluralist. If I am a Christian exclusivist and discover after death that Hick's version of pluralism really is true, I will have lost nothing except Hick's good will during this life. But if I am a pluralist and it turns out that Christian exclusivism is true, then the consequences for me will be very serious. Pluralism places much capital at great risk.

## DOES HICK HAVE A HIDDEN RELIGIOUS AGENDA?

John Hick still describes himself as a "Christian" in the loose, essentially contentless sense that the term holds for many people today. Yet I mean no ill-will when I say that Hick is not a Christian in any historical, traditional, or biblical sense of the word. This is not being unkind; it is only being accurate.

But more attention needs to be given to the extremely vague contours of the religious system Hick is recommending. Some observers of Hick's recent work have noted how closely his basic ideas resemble certain Eastern ways of talking about Ultimate Reality. At the end of chapter 2, I highlighted Hick's advocacy of Eastern religious thought with Hick's own comparison of Buddhist *sunyata* to the Real and then noted Doug Geivett's analysis.

Because of Hick's shaky "Christianity," Geivett feels that more attention should be given to the impact of Hick's pluralism on people who have doubts about their own religious heritage.

> It would seem that many religious believers could only accept the pluralistic hypothesis at the cost of drastically reconceiving the nature of their own particular faith tradition. This, of course, is precisely what John Hick has done himself.[12]

One of my purposes thus far has been to reveal the high price that must be paid by any evangelical Protestant or traditional Roman Catholic who may feel attracted to pluralism or who, at least, feels moved by some of its claims. Any Christians who would become pluralists must cease being Christians. They must also, for that matter, commit themselves to what amounts to a version of a non-Christian faith. But the same price must be paid by Jewish and Muslim believers who might feel attracted to pluralism. While pluralism's natural home is a small set of offshoots of the larger Eastern religions, the majority of devotees will find that movement toward pluralism will require them also to accept major distortions of their faith.

## CONCLUSION

John Hick has a prominent standing among those who teach and write about the major world religions. He also speaks as a self-professed "Christian" intellectual. This explains why many people's ideas about Christianity and the world religions are being filtered through the grid of Hick's theories. Hick's approach to Christianity and religion is presented to many college and seminary students as brilliant, compassionate, and tolerant. For this reason, Hick's ideas are having a far greater influence than they deserve. One hopes that Hick's views will be examined ever more carefully and that the unstable foundations of his theory will lead to a more realistic and justly negative evaluation of his claims.

---

12. Geivett, "John Hick's Approach to Religious Pluralism," 50.

# PART TWO

# INCLUSIVISM

Chapter Seven

# AN INTRODUCTION
# TO INCLUSIVISM

Inclusivists see their position as a middle ground between exclusivism and pluralism that preserves the most important insights of the other two views. Inclusivists agree with pluralists that God's salvation is not restricted to the relatively few people who hear the gospel and believe in Jesus Christ. Inclusivists agree with exclusivists that God's universally accessible salvation is nonetheless grounded on the person of Jesus Christ and his redemptive work.

Gavin D'Costa, a Roman Catholic inclusivist, states that his view "affirms the salvific presence of God in non-Christian religions while still maintaining that Christ is the definitive and authoritative revelation of God."[1] Pluralist John Hick's description of inclusivism presents it as the belief that "God's forgiveness and acceptance off humanity have been made possible by Christ's death, but . . . the benefits of this sacrifice are not confined to those who respond to it with an explicit act of faith."[2] According to Alan Race, inclusivism "accepts the spiritual

---

1. Gavin D'Costa, *Theology and Religious Pluralism* (New York: Basil Blackwell, 1986), 80.

2. John Hick, "A Philosophy of Religious Pluralism," in *The World's Religious Traditions: Current Perspectives in Religious Studies. Essays in Honour of Wilfred Cantwell Smith,* ed. F. Whaling (Edinburgh: T. & T. Clark, 1984), 152.

power and depth manifest in [other religions], so that they can properly be called a locus of divine presence. On the other hand, it rejects them as not being sufficient for salvation apart from Christ, for Christ alone is saviour."[3]

Part of inclusivism's appeal is its response to the problem of dealing with the millions of people who die without ever hearing the gospel. Inclusivists insist that all people must have a chance to be saved. They teach "that God, in grace, grants every individual a genuine opportunity to participate in the redemptive work of the Lord Jesus, that no human being is excluded from the possibility of benefiting from salvific grace."[4] As John Sanders explains,

> [T]he unevangelized are saved or lost on the basis of their commitment, or lack thereof, to the God who saves through the work of Jesus. [Inclusivists] believe that appropriation of salvific grace is mediated through general revelation and God's providential workings in human history. Briefly, inclusivists affirm the particularity and finality of salvation only in Christ but deny that knowledge of his work is necessary for salvation — [T]he work of Jesus is ontologically necessary for salvation (no one would be saved without it) but not epistemologically necessary (one need not be aware of the work in order to benefit from it).[5]

While pluralists believe that sincere followers of non-Christian religions can experience salvation through those religions, inclusivists insist that devout believers in other religions will be saved, but only on the basis of Christ's atoning work.

## THE TWO AXIOMS OF INCLUSIVISM

Inclusivists speak often of two axioms, or presuppositions, that serve as starting points for their theory.

---

3. Alan Race, *Christians and Religious Pluralism* (Maryknoll, N.Y.: Orbis Books, 1982), 38.

4. John Sanders, *No Other Name* (Grand Rapids: Eerdmans, 1992), 131.

5. Ibid., 215.

## "The Particularity Axiom"

The particularity axiom focuses on Jesus Christ as the only mediator of salvation. Clark Pinnock affirms "the uniqueness and finality of Jesus Christ and [regards] as heretical any attempt to reduce or water down this conviction."[6] According to Pinnock, the central Christian conviction about the lordship of Christ "is nonnegotiable for Christians and has to be seen as a basic rule of Christian speech."[7] Christians cannot possibly regard the lordship of Christ "as a bargaining chip in an interreligious dialogue."[8] Further, "Christians ought to confess that Jesus was and is the unique vehicle and means of God's saving love in the world, and its definitive Savior — All religions make absolute claims at some point, and Christians ought to make them in the matter of the finality of Jesus Christ."[9] This belief about the finality of Jesus must not be watered down, inclusivists insist.

## "The Universality Axiom"

By the term "universality axiom," inclusivists mean that God intends his salvation to be available to all humans (1 Tim. 2:4; Titus 2:11). Inclusivists sometimes treat two propositions as synonymous: (1) the claim that God wills the salvation of every human being, and (2) the claim that God gives every human a chance to accept his grace. It ought to be obvious, however, that even if (1) were true, it would not follow that (2) is true.

The "universality axiom" does entail the inclusivist's belief that "There is a wonderful broadness in the apparent narrowness of the Christian confession."[10] Sanders spells this out: "the salvation God so magnanimously gives is, and has been, available in every age and culture and spot on the globe apart from

---

6. Clark H. Pinnock, "The Finality of Jesus Christ in a World of Religions," in *Christian Faith and Practice in the Modern World*, ed. Mark A. Noll and David F. Wells (Grand Rapids: Eerdmans, 1988), 153.

7. Ibid., 155.

8. Ibid.

9. Ibid.

10. Pinnock, "The Finality of Jesus Christ," 157.

any specific knowledge of God's historical activity in Israel and in his son Jesus."[11]

### Summary

Inclusivists believe their two axioms complement each other. The "universality axiom" expresses their belief that God must make salvation available to all human beings, including everyone who lived before Christ outside the sphere of Jewish influence and everyone since Christ who has lived without hearing about the gospel. This humanwide emphasis is then focused in the "particularity axiom" on the one and only Mediator whose person and redemptive work is the ground for salvation.

## INCLUSIVISM AND EVANGELICALISM

Evangelicals are Christian believers whose theology is traditional or orthodox as defined by the historic Christian creeds. They also take the Bible as their ultimate authority in matters of faith and practice, have had a religious conversion, and are interested in leading others to the same kind of conversion experience.[12] Clark Pinnock and John Sanders are inclusivists as well as evangelicals.

Part of the initial distrust many evangelicals feel on their first encounter with inclusivism results no doubt from their inability to sort out differences with clearly nonevangelical positions such as universalism and pluralism. After all, evangelicals take Christ's Great Commission seriously and they are likely to be confused when they hear other evangelicals telling them that large numbers of unevangelized people will be saved.

The number of evangelicals who are sympathetic to inclusivism may be larger than many think. John Sanders, for example, cites statistics from a 1975 InterVarsity conference at the University of Illinois at Urbana that suggests that as many as 25

---

11. Sanders, *No Other Name*, 216.
12. Anyone familiar with the subject will recognize that such a sentence is just a starting point for defining evangelicalism. For more, see Ronald Nash, *Evangelicals in America* (Nashville: Abingdon, 1987).

percent of people active in Christian service at that time held to some variant of inclusivism.[13] Sanders is persuaded that the percentage of inclusivists today would be much larger. My own observation of evangelical leaders in places of denominational or missions leadership along with professors at mainstream evangelical colleges and seminaries points to a number higher than 50 percent. Among college and seminary professors in my own denomination, the Southern Baptist Convention, the number would be even higher.[14]

Although the number of evangelical laypeople sympathetic to inclusivism is probably much smaller, it would not surprise me if a third or more of nonprofessionals in evangelical churches expressed support for inclusivist convictions. It is difficult to know what conclusions to draw from this. Until inclusivists like Pinnock and Sanders published their books in the early 1990s, few evangelicals had any opportunity to think through the significant biblical and theological issues at stake. Now that the inclusivists have expressed their views publicly, the critical evaluations of their thinking that are bound to appear may help to sharpen the debate and inform evangelicals who may be attracted to inclusivism initially with their hearts rather than their minds.

If the issue is framed solely or primarily in terms of the plight of the unevangelized, we might expect to find theologically untrained Christians offering opinions that appear to support inclusivism. But it remains to be seen how their response might differ should they realize the consequences of inclusivism for Scripture and Christian theology.

John Sanders points to a number of twentieth-century evangelicals as likely adherents of inclusivism. His list includes G. Campbell Morgan, Edward John Carnell, C. S. Lewis, Bernard

---

13. See Sanders, *No Other Name,* 216, fn. 1.

14. As the leadership of the Southern Baptist Convention has turned in an increasingly conservative direction since 1980, the earlier sympathy with inclusivism that pervaded the higher layers of the denomination's leadership has declined significantly. As this conservative trend affects seminary boards, one may expect to see some slight modifications downward among seminary faculty. But college faculty in this denomination are less likely to change because the colleges are much less reflective of the beliefs of local churches.

Ramm, D. Bruce Lockerbie, George E. Ladd, William Dyrness, J. Herbert Kane, and J. N. D. Anderson among others.[15] Including some of these people might be misleading, however, because they expressed apparently inclusivist opinions only in passing and in a context that was more theologically ambiguous than now. But there is nothing ambiguous about this statement by evangelical author, Stuart Hackett, who taught for many years at Wheaton College and at Trinity Evangelical Divinity School:

> If every human being in all times and ages has been objectively provided for through the unique redemption in Jesus, and if this provision is in fact intended by God for every such human being, then it must be possible for every human individual to become personally eligible to receive that provision — regardless of his historical, cultural, or personal circumstances and situation, and quite apart from any particular historical information or even historically formulated theological conceptualisation — since a universally intended redemptive provision is not genuinely universal unless it is also and for that reason universally accessible.[16]

Putting aside for now any discussion of Hackett's last statement, we find in this paragraph dramatic testimony to the influence inclusivism has today in centers of evangelical higher education. Yet we should note that just because some evangelical leaders *claim* that their movement is compatible with inclusivism, it does not follow that those leaders are necessarily correct. The search for an answer to this issue is a major task of this book.

## INCLUSIVISM AND THE CONTEMPORARY ROMAN CATHOLIC CHURCH

Although inclusivism is at best a minority position within the whole of the Protestant evangelical movement, it is the view of a majority of Roman Catholic thinkers. Indeed, a movement toward inclusivism is one of the major legacies of Vatican

---

15. See Sanders, *No Other Name,* 274 – 80.
16. Stuart C. Hackett, *The Reconstruction of the Christian Revelation Claim* (Grand Rapids: Baker, 1984), 244.

Council II (1962 – 65), which issued a statement declaring that "They also can attain to everlasting salvation who through no fault of their own do not know the gospel of Christ or his church, yet sincerely seek God, and moved by grace, strive by their deeds to do his will as it is known to them through the dictates of conscience."[17] If our examination uncovers reasons to question Protestant inclusivism, they should apply to Roman Catholic inclusivism as well.

The best-known and most influential Catholic inclusivist is Karl Rahner (1904 – 1984), a German theologian. In his own way, Rahner embraced both the particular and universal axioms. In his words, "God desires the salvation of everyone [the universality axiom] and this salvation willed by God is the salvation won by Christ [the particularity axiom]."[18]

Rahner believed that human nature includes an openness to the divine that lies beyond us. Grace is not something to be added to our human nature; instead, it defines our nature. Human knowing and loving are but two ways of reaching beyond ourselves toward the Infinite Mystery that is God.[19] Michael Barnes explains Rahner's thinking this way: "Every time we reach out beyond ourselves to the True and the Good we are experiencing and responding to grace; we are therefore in some sense knowing God even if such a knowledge must be described as . . . implicit rather than explicit."[20]

While a non-Christian religion may possess validity prior to its encounter with the gospel, Rahner states, that validity is subject to a specific time limit. Once the Christian gospel confronts a non-Christian religion, enters into the culture of the people who once adhered to the religion, and becomes embodied in community, that other religion ceases to be valid. Rahner believed that God's offer of grace is mediated through the non-Christian religions.[21] "Christianity," Rahner argues, "does not simply confront

17. Vatican II, *Dogmatic Constitution of the Church*, Par. 16.
18. Karl Rahner, *Theological Investigations* (New York: Seabury, 1966), 5:122.
19. See Karl Rahner, *Revelation and Tradition* (New York: Herder and Herder, 1966), 122, and his *Theological Investigations*, 6:390 – 98.
20. Michael Barnes, *Christian Identity and Religious Pluralism* (Nashville: Abingdon, 1989), 52.
21. See Rahner's *Theological Investigations*, 5:121.

the member of an extra-Christian religion as a mere non-Christian but as someone who can and must already be regarded in this or that respect as an anonymous Christian. It would be wrong to regard the pagan as someone who has not yet been touched in any way by God's grace and truth."[22]

Even before such non-Christians have been affected externally through missionary activity, they have already received something of God's revelation internally, according to Rahner. "[T]he proclamation of the Gospel," he writes, "does not simply turn someone absolutely abandoned by God and Christ into a Christian, but turns an anonymous Christian into someone who now also knows about his Christian belief in the depths of his grace-endowed being by objective reflection and in the profession of faith which is given a social form in the Church."[23]

What occurs in the transformation of non-Christians described by Rahner is quite unlike the evangelical understanding of conversion. Gavin D'Costa explains, "It is not simply a matter of making explicit what was only implicit before, but being transformed, moulded and nourished by the social and historical particulars of the liturgy, worship, and sacramental structures of the [Roman Catholic] Church."[24]

Rahner denied that his inclusivism compromises the Christian church's historical understanding of itself "as the absolute religion, intended for all men, which cannot recognize any religion besides itself as of equal right."[25] At the same time, he refused to deny the lawful character of non-Christian religions that can be and, indeed, are used by God in preparing anonymous Christians for his grace. The errors of the religions are still there, but God mediates his offer of grace through these non-Christian faiths. Yet Rahner failed to suggest specific ways as to how this divine mediation of grace actually happens.

We say all this in order to understand Rahner's phrase "anonymous Christian," by which he means "a non-Christian who gains salvation through faith, hope, and love by the grace

---

22. Ibid., 5:131.
23. Ibid., 5:132.
24. D'Costa, *Theology and Religious Pluralism*, 88.
25. Rahner, *Theological Investigations*, 5:118.

of Christ, mediated however imperfectly through his or her own religion, which thereby points towards its historical fulfillment in Christ and his Church."[26]

John B. Cobb, Jr., sums up the heart of Rahner's inclusivism. According to Rahner,

> God works salvifically everywhere. People can be saved whether or not they are related to the Catholic church or consciously accept Jesus Christ. People saved in this way he calls anonymous Christians. The religions of the world are used by God in this salvific work. Thus they are positive vehicles of salvation. But they are not on a par with the Christian church. Once the Christian church is fully established in a community there is no longer any need for other religions there. Their function in the history of salvation is superseded by that of the Christian church.[27]

Rahner's term "anonymous Christian" has now become part of our contemporary theological vocabulary. But Rahner's belief that sincere Hindus and Muslims may prove to be anonymous Christians has not endeared his work to noninclusivists in these other traditions. Pluralist John Hick dismisses Rahner's position as simply another Christian epicycle, that is, "an attempt to accommodate growing knowledge of other faiths by drawing a more complicated, but still thoroughly Christianity-centered map."[28] As Hick sees it, Rahner's position lacks credibility: "When salvation is acknowledged to be taking place without any connection with the Christian Church or Gospel, in people who are living on the basis of quite other faiths, is it not a somewhat empty gesture to insist upon fixing a Christian label to them?"[29]

So, while pluralists dismiss Rahner's work as an offensive Christian paternalism that fails to give enough credit to non-

26. Gavin D'Costa, *John Hick's Theology of Religions* (Lanham, Md.: University Press of America, 1987), 35.

27. John B. Cobb, Jr., "The Meaning of Pluralism for Christian Self-Understanding," in *Religious Pluralism*, ed. Leroy S. Rouner (South Bend, Ind.: University of Notre Dame Press, 1984), 165.

28. I derived this point from Michael Barnes, *Christian Identity and Religious Pluralism*, 73.

29. Hick, "A Philosophy of Religious Pluralism," 153.

Christian religions, conservatives fault Rahner for giving other religions too much credit. If Rahner were even close to being right, they argue, it ought to be possible to see large numbers of "righteous" non-Christians moving toward Christ. This is hardly what we do in fact observe. Exclusivists also fault Rahner as to the place of Christian missions and the role of the Christian church. Moreover, they maintain, Rahner's view compromises preaching about Jesus Christ; Christian discipleship loses its distinctive character; the cross of Christ loses its centrality.

Evangelical theologian Clark Pinnock seeks to distance himself from what he regards as the "rosy-eyed optimism" that has "tended to lead Roman Catholic scholars down the path toward relativism." Pinnock describes himself as wanting "to be more realistic about the good and evil in religions and not be naive when it comes to building bridges and engaging in dialogue."[30] He also objects to Rahner's notion of anonymous Christians as going much too far "in the direction of sanctifying non-Christian religions as vehicles of salvation in the lives of those who call out to God from within paganism."[31] In Pinnock's view, Rahner writes as if being a Buddhist is perfectly all right. We must not say anything, Pinnock contends, that would create the impression that some people do not need to repent and believe the gospel.[32]

## EVANGELICAL INCLUSIVISM
## AND NON-CHRISTIAN RELIGIONS

Pinnock's words hold out the promise that the evangelical inclusivists will exhibit a more realistic attitude toward non-Christian religions than one finds among post-Vatican II Roman Catholics. Is that promise fulfilled?

On the one hand, Pinnock declares that "it is possible to appreciate positive elements in other faiths, recognizing that God has been at work among them."[33] This leads Pinnock to observe

---

30. Clark Pinnock, "Toward an Evangelical Theology of Religions," *Journal of the Evangelical Theological Society* 33 (1990): 368.

31. Pinnock, "The Finality of Jesus Christ in a World of Religions," 164.

32. Pinnock admits that Rahner did not intend to leave this impression. Nonetheless, this is how he has been understood.

33. Clark Pinnock, *A Wideness in God's Mercy* (Grand Rapids: Zondervan, 1992), 97.

that "If people in Ghana speak of the transcendent God as the shining one, as unchangeable as a rock, as all-wise and all-loving, how can anyone conclude otherwise than that they intend to acknowledge the true God as we do?"[34]

Pinnock seems much too generous in this matter. It tends toward the "rosy-eyed optimism" that he finds distasteful in Roman Catholic inclusivism. One wonders how he can describe the Ghanian's god in terms of "transcendence," a complex theological concept, with roots in Aquinas and Augustine, that can be difficult to explain. Imputing transcendence to the object of a Ghanian's religious devotion appears to be a case of wishful thinking, as is Pinnock's confidence that a similarity here or there *proves* that the Ghanian's god is identical with the sovereign, triune, and holy God of Scripture. Even people sympathetic to the inclusivists' agenda are likely to be embarrassed by such zeal in the search for religious parallels.

Regarding Buddhism, Pinnock writes, "We must not conclude, just because we know a person to be a Buddhist, that his or her heart is not seeking God."[35] Even as we grant this, the Bible does speak of people whose quest for the Ultimate leads them to seek after false gods. Pinnock anticipates this caveat in declaring, "What God really cares about is faith and not theology, trust and not orthodoxy."[36]

This is a crucial point for Pinnock that will require further analysis later on. He is working here with a commonly held distinction between the subjective and objective components of faith.

Evangelicals typically argue that two things are required for saving faith: (1) Faith must be directed toward the right object, and (2) the proper object of faith must be approached with certain subjective attitudes, including sincerity and genuine commitment. Many church members can recite a set of creedal statements without exhibiting the slightest degree of sorrow over their sins or personal commitment to Jesus Christ. Such people embrace the objective component of faith right, but fall

34. Ibid., 97.
35. Ibid., 112.
36. Ibid., 112.

short on the subjective commitment. Pinnock seems to be saying that if people have the subjective side of faith right (sincerity, perhaps, or intensity or a truly seeking attitude), it is irrelevant that those subjective attitudes turn out to be directed toward a false god.

Pinnock draws attention to one Hindu sect that, he says, "celebrates a personal God of love." The literature of this sect "expresses the belief that all God's actions in the world are intended to express love for his creatures and to lead them into loving union with himself."[37] One wishes that Pinnock had provided sufficient examples to demonstrate that he was not too quickly reading his own Christian beliefs into this literature.

Pinnock has equally positive thoughts about the Japanese sect known as Shin-Shu Amida, which includes an emphasis on grace and faith. Once again, one wonders whether Pinnock is not moving too quickly. The fact that a sect seems to say that "salvation"[38] is given to humans as a gift and not as a reward hardly bridges the gulf between it and the New Testament notion of grace, which is showered upon rebellious sinners who are utterly helpless to save themselves. Even Pinnock must admit that all-important differences exist.

It is not my intention to denigrate the non-Christian beliefs discussed or to offend people devoted to those faiths. Anyone, including Pinnock and me, would want to avoid distorting anyone's beliefs in order to make a point. Many Christians will think that Pinnock is distorting important elements of *their* beliefs to make his case for inclusivism appear more plausible. But I believe that the parallels and analogies Pinnock offers do not really establish anything. When he asks, "how does one come away after encountering Buddhism and deny that it is in touch with God in its way?"[39] I am left wondering what he is talking about. Many Buddhists do not believe in any god at all, and others do not believe in a transcendent, personal God.

---

37. Ibid., 100.
38. It should be noted that Pinnock in this context provides absolutely no clue as to what "salvation" means and what connection it might have with human sin.
39. Pinnock, *A Wideness in God's Mercy,* 100.

What about the inclusivist idea that other religions can and do exhibit some similarities with Christianity? We need to look carefully at the full context of those beliefs. The weighty differences are hardly irrelevant.

## INCLUSIVISM AND UNIVERSALISM

To whatever degree evangelicals find inclusivism disappointing or problematic, they will at least appreciate the evangelical inclusivist's clear disavowal of universalism, the belief that all humans will eventually be saved.

Inclusivist arguments against universalism stress two points. First, universalism lacks biblical support. The biblical texts that universalists cite as teaching God's intent to save all humans turn out to affirm nothing more than the inclusivist's belief in a universally accessible salvation. "[A]lthough Calvary was for all," John Sanders writes, "salvation is only for believers."[40]

Second, universalism cannot do justice to the biblical teaching of hell. Clark Pinnock argues, "There are too many warnings about divine judgment falling on people to be ignored, warnings that suggest that rejection [of God] is possible."[41] Even though his warning about hell is muted somewhat by his belief in the annihilation of the sinner, Pinnock does believe that many humans will reject God's offer of salvation and suffer eternal loss.[42] He dismisses universalism as an example of wishful thinking that ignores the many judgment passages in Scripture referring to the destruction of the wicked.

All of this clarifies an important and reassuring point: Christian inclusivists are not universalists.[43]

---

40. Sanders, *No Other Name*, 107.

41. Pinnock, *A Wideness in God's Mercy*, 156.

42. For more detail on Pinnock's view of hell as annihilation along with other views of the doctrine, see William Crockett, ed., *Four Views on Hell* (Grand Rapids: Zondervan, 1992).

43. For much more detail about universalism, see Sanders, *No Other Name*, chap. 3.

## CONCLUSION

In this introduction to inclusivism we have learned that many Roman Catholics and some evangelical Protestants believe that sincere, God-fearing adherents of non-Christian religions will be saved, even though they may die without hearing the gospel. But inclusivists disagree with universalists, who teach that all human beings will eventually be saved. Inclusivists also disagree with pluralists, who teach that non-Christian religions offer genuine salvation. If non-Christians are saved, inclusivists insist, they can only be saved on the basis of the person and work of Jesus Christ, the only Savior.

In the next two chapters I will examine specific disagreements between inclusivists and exclusivists. Chapter 8 will explore theological issues, and chapter 9 will focus on differences over what the Bible teaches.

# Chapter Eight

# INCLUSIVISM AND THEOLOGY

In chapters 8 and 9 I examine most of the arguments, both theological and biblical, that inclusivists offer in support of their position. The theological arguments come first for pedagogical reasons, that is, my considerations introduce information that help our understanding of inclusivism. But despite the separation of chapters, no strict segregation of the biblical and theological issues is really possible. Once we raise the theological issues, we must take a hard look at what the Scriptures say about them.

## GENERAL REVELATION

Christian thinkers distinguish between special and general revelation. Special revelation is illustrated by the unique disclosures that God made to such people as Abraham, Moses, and Paul. This kind of revelation is "special" because God gave it to particular people at particular times and places. This revelation also has a special function, namely, to bring human beings to a saving relationship with the triune God. Because some of the content of special revelation that God gave to select individuals like David and Peter was not preserved and recorded, that material is not accessible to us today. Special revelation that is accessible has been preserved, recorded, and inscripturated in the Bible. Since Jesus Christ is God incarnate, his life and teachings also constitute special revelation. But again, our access to that important information is limited to what has been preserved in Scripture.

General revelation, as its name implies, is revelation that God makes available to all human beings. Psalm 19 tells us that the heavens declare the glory of God. The last half of Romans 1 reports that humans can come to know certain things about the Creator God through his creation. General revelation also gives humans general moral understanding so that certain kinds of conduct are known to be wrong.

A key assumption of inclusivism is the belief that general revelation is sufficient to bring people to salvation. Inclusivists *have* to say this. They insist that salvation is accessible to all humans, including the millions who lack any contact with special revelation. Because special revelation is not necessary for salvation in such cases, inclusivists are forced to find a salvific role in a general revelation that all humans can apprehend. Clark Pinnock states that "the knowledge of God is not limited to places where biblical revelation has penetrated."[1] According to John Sanders, inclusivists "believe that appropriation of salvific grace is mediated through general revelation and God's providential workings in human history."[2]

Sanders insists that the word *gospel* has a wider meaning than simply the good news about Jesus. The gospel may also include light that is available to the unevangelized through general revelation. One obvious problem with such a claim is its apparent conflict with Paul's words in 1 Corinthians 15:3 – 4, where Paul seems to unfold the meaning of "gospel" in terms of Christ's death, burial, and resurrection. Sanders's answer to this difficulty amounts to a watering down of Paul's words. He claims that "Paul does not say one has to know these facts [about Christ's death and resurrection] to be saved, only that he had proclaimed this message to the Corinthians."[3]

To protect their particular view of general revelation, inclusivists have to relativize the content of Paul's gospel to different people, places, and times. This condition should give evangelicals second thoughts about embracing inclusivism. As we saw

---

1. Clark H. Pinnock, "The Finality of Jesus Christ in a World of Religions," in *Christian Faith and Practice in the Modern World*, ed. Mark A. Noll and David F. Wells (Grand Rapids: Eerdmans, 1988), 159.

2. John Sanders, *No Other Name* (Grand Rapids: Eerdmans, 1992), 215.

3. Ibid., 255.

with pluralism, so with inclusivism: Ideas have consequences. Is the death and resurrection of Jesus essential to the gospel, or is the gospel instead an assortment of things that can assume many different forms? As we will discover, Sanders's response to 1 Corinthians 15:3 – 4 is typical of how inclusivists handle most biblical passages that appear to conflict with important inclusivist convictions. In many cases, what Christians have historically regarded as a significant New Testament passage testifying to Christ's exclusive role as Savior is watered down so that it becomes a trivial or unimportant utterance.

### *Does Romans 1 – 3 Contradict the Inclusivist View of General Revelation?*

Paul begins his letter to the Romans by explaining that one reason why all humans are condemned is that they have resisted the message of general revelation. Romans 1:18 – 19 states, "The wrath of God is being revealed from heaven against all the godlessness and wickedness of men who suppress the truth by their wickedness, since what may be known about God is plain to them, because God has made it plain to them." Even though God has made important information available to all humans through general revelation, Paul teaches, that revelation has failed to bring about salvation. "There is no one righteous, not even one," Paul writes in Romans 3:10. "[A]ll have sinned and fall short of the glory of God" (Rom. 3:23). Romans 1 – 3 seems clearly to contradict the inclusivist belief that people in non-Christian religions may be saved by responding in faith to the content of general revelation.[4] Paul makes it plain that general revelation does not and cannot save.

Bruce Demarest summarizes what is generally taken to be Paul's teaching:

> We have seen that through universal general revelation God has disclosed to people His existence, perfections, and moral demands. But we have also seen that sinful man consistently repudiates this elemental knowledge of God and perverts it

---

4. As we will see, even this declaration about non-Christians responding to the *content* of general revelation turns out to be too generous. Inclusivists like Pinnock question whether saving faith requires *any* cognitive content at all.

into unspeakable idolatry. Thus, in practice, general revelation serves only to condemn man, not to save him. However, the God of grace and mercy did not abandon the sinner in his state of self-willed rebellion. God has broken into man's sin-darkened existence with a special supernatural revelation that holds out the offer of spiritual healing. By this fresh revelatory initiative, God offers Himself to man not only as a power to be encountered but as a Person to be known in a fellowship of trust and commitment.[5]

Paul's teaching that no human being succeeds in living up to the light of general revelation implies that general revelation cannot save; special revelation is required for that result. In response to this point Sanders appeals to the fact that "Paul also says that all the Jews, who had special revelation, have sinned and that *none* of them seeks God either." In other words, the exclusivist appeal to Romans 1 – 3 "appears to lead to the conclusion that since none of us seeks God, no matter what sort of revelation we have, *all people* are damned to hell."[6]

Sanders's argument is not entirely clear. He reasons that because exclusivists, on the basis of Paul's writings, reject general revelation as a vehicle of salvation, they should also disdain special revelation because it failed to bring every Jew to saving faith. This is a very weak argument. The exclusivist believes that while general revelation saves no one, God's special revelation has been effectual in saving many Jews, including Paul. Furthermore, Scripture does affirm the salvific sufficiency of special revelation when coupled with the effectual work of the Holy Spirit (1 Cor. 2). Paul's words in Romans 2:17 – 24 do not give general revelation enhanced status as an instrument of salvation. Romans 1 – 3 still contradicts the inclusivist view of general revelation.

### Alleged Proof Texts for the Inclusivist Position

Inclusivists need some clear and strong support from Scripture to ground their belief in the salvific function of general revelation. John Sanders finds that support in Romans 10:18:

---

5. Bruce A. Demarest, *General Revelation* (Grand Rapids: Zondervan, 1982), 248.
6. Sanders, *No Other Name*, 69.

"Did they not hear? Of course they did.'Their voice has gone out into all the earth, their words to the ends of the world.'" The key part of the verse for inclusivists is Paul's quotation from Psalm 19:4. Admittedly, these words are a poetical allusion to the power of general revelation. Who can forget the first verse of that Psalm and its message: "The heavens declare the glory of God; the skies proclaim the work of his hands"?

However, inclusivists overreach when they call Paul's use of Psalm 19:4 an endorsement of a salvific role for general revelation. New Testament scholar F. F. Bruce explains, "It is unnecessary to suppose that Paul regarded Psalm xix. 4 as a *prediction* of the world-wide dissemination of the gospel; he means that the dissemination of the gospel is becoming as world-wide as the light of the heavenly bodies."[7] If the inclusivist view were true, it would bring Paul's entire argument in that chapter to an abrupt halt. Even the most superficial reading of the context makes it clear that Paul is talking about the indispensability of special revelation for salvation and the urgency of human preachers to carry the gospel to the world. Romans 10 is exalting special, not general, revelation.

D. Bruce Lockerbie interprets Romans 2:14 – 16 in a way that seems to support inclusivism. For him, this passage teaches that some Gentiles do acknowledge God and obey his will. Such people will be saved on judgment day, but not because they lived sinless lives. On the contrary, these Gentiles will also have fallen short of the high standard set for them by God's moral law. These saved Gentiles, Lockerbie explains, "will be devout pagans who, in the presence of sin, have been ashamed, have cried out in spiritual anguish, and confessed to whatever representation of the Holy Spirit they acknowledge."[8] The problem is, Romans 2:14 – 16 says nothing about pagan Gentiles who seek salvation because of guilty consciences, and it certainly says nothing about their search being successful. The passage only talks about those times when some unevangelized people

7. F. F. Bruce, *The Epistle of Paul to the Romans* (Grand Rapids: Eerdmans, 1963), 209.

8. D. Bruce Lockerbie, *The Cosmic Center* (Portland, Oreg.: Multnomah Press, 1986), 176.

experience guilt because of their failure to meet the standards of the moral law that God has placed within all human beings. Romans 2:14 – 16 does not support the inclusivist view of general revelation.

The final text inclusivists appeal to regarding the salvific sufficiency of general revelation is John 1:9, which describes Jesus Christ, the Logos of God, as "The true light that gives light to every man." It is not at all clear that this verse has anything directly to do with salvation. As I have argued at length in two other books, the verse describes God's role in endowing humans with rationality and the ability to attain knowledge.[9] Nothing in John 1:9 gives inclusivists the help they need.

Where, then, is the clear, unambiguous biblical support inclusivists need for their belief in the salvific function of general revelation? The simple answer is that there is none. The inclusivist's view of general revelation is assumed without biblical warrant and is then used to compromise other important biblical teachings such as Paul's identification of Christ's death and resurrection as an essential component of the gospel. So although inclusivists want desperately to believe that general revelation can bring humans to salvation, they fail to show that Scripture teaches this view and fail to recognize a conflict with Paul's teaching in Romans 1 – 3.

## THE DISTINCTION
## BETWEEN CHRISTIANS AND BELIEVERS

Throughout this chapter I argue that accepting inclusivism logically commits a person to a number of other positions that many people who are otherwise attracted to inclusivism find problematic. The inclusivist view of general revelation is only one of them. We turn now to another set of issues, all related to the fact that inclusivists are compelled by the logic of their theory to make a distinction between Christians and believers. John

---

9. See Ronald Nash, *The Gospel and the Greeks* (Dallas: Probe Books, 1992) and *The Word of God and the Mind of Man* (Phillipsburg, N.J.: Presbyterian and Reformed, 1992).

Sanders defines believers "as all those who are saved because they have faith in God."[10] A Christian, by contrast, is "a believer who knows about and participates in the work of Jesus Christ."[11] This means that in heaven we will encounter both Christian and non-Christian believers. This view is inherent in inclusivism.

This theory is supported by three claims that are inseparable from inclusivism: (1) a distinctively inclusivist understanding of the nature of faith; (2) a recognition that the many Old Testament believers will be in heaven, even though they were not *Christian* believers. (Hence, inclusivists argue, the Bible itself makes a distinction between Christians and believers. Because the Old Testament establishes the principle that there will be believers in heaven who are not Christians, the possibility exists of there being other believers in heaven who are not Christians, namely, unevangelized believers from non-Christian religions.); (3) an appeal to an alleged Old Testament tradition of so-called holy pagans.

Let us deal now with these three claims and then return to the question of whether a distinction between believers and Christians is defensible.

## THE INCLUSIVIST UNDERSTANDING OF FAITH

While inclusivists believe that an act of faith is necessary for salvation, they insist that this faith need not have Jesus as its direct object. Many Christians will find this view strange. Consider the following quotations from John Sanders:

> [P]eople can receive the gift of salvation without knowing the giver or the precise nature of the gift.[12]

> "Saving faith" . . . does not necessitate knowledge of Christ in this life. God's gracious activity is wider than the arena of special revelation. God will accept into his kingdom those who repent and trust him even if they know nothing of Jesus.[13]

---

10. John Sanders, *No Other Name*, 224–25.

11. Ibid., 225.

12. Ibid., 255.

13. John E. Sanders, "Is Belief in Christ Necessary for Salvation?" *Evangelical Quarterly* 60 (1988): 252–53.

> [I]nclusivism denies that Jesus must be the object of saving
> faith.[14]

Inclusivists obviously believe the salvation of unevangelized people depends on how they respond to the light they
have. In ways that inclusivists find difficult to explain, the light
of general revelation brings many of the unevangelized to a
trust in the true God, a trust that has nothing to do with Jesus
Christ, of whom they are uninformed.

According to Clark Pinnock, people are saved by what he
calls "the faith principle." That is, the saved must satisfy the
conditions of Hebrews 11:6: "Without faith it is impossible to
please God, because anyone who comes to him must believe
that he exists and that he rewards those who earnestly seek
him." It is faith or trust that saves, not knowledge. But does
Hebrews 11:6 exhaust the content of faith? Obviously one pre-
condition for saving faith is believing that God exists. Just as
certainly, believers are expected to "seek" God, although other
passages in the Bible will have to give this "seeking" the proper
content. This much we can learn from Hebrews 11:6.

But I do not think that is all there is to saving faith. Surely
this faith in the existence of God must be directed to the true
God, not some idol or pagan substitute. The New Testament
clearly states that humans who would seek God must approach
him through the one and only mediator, Jesus Christ (1 Tim.
2:15). The "Faith Principle" that Pinnock formulates from
Hebrews 11:6 is incomplete; it distorts and dilutes the New
Testament's picture of saving faith.

### What About the Content of Saving Faith?

Clark Pinnock declares that "According to the Bible, people
are saved by faith, not by the content of their theology."[15] An inclusivist has no choice but to make this claim. If God saves people solely on the basis of "faith," irrespective of their access to
special revelation, the gospel, and Jesus Christ, then an inclu-

---

14. Sanders, *No Other Name*, 265.
15. Clark Pinnock, *A Wideness in God's Mercy* (Grand Rapids: Zondervan,
1992), 157.

sivist's view of saving faith will be radically different from the traditional evangelical view. Apart from having the true God as its object, the key factor about saving faith in inclusivist terms is its subjective aspect. Note these statements by Pinnock:

> "Faith in God is what saves, not possessing certain minimum information."[16]

> "A person is saved by faith, even if the content of faith is deficient (and whose is not?). The Bible does not teach that one must confess the name of Jesus to be saved."[17]

> "One does not have to be conscious of the work of Christ done on one's behalf in order to benefit from that work. The issue God cares about is the direction of the heart, not the content of theology."[18]

When I was growing up in Ohio, I frequently heard liberal pastors proclaim sentiments identical to those now expressed by evangelical inclusivists: "It's not *what* you believe that matters, it's your sincerity that counts."[19]

Pinnock remains an evangelical. But it bears notice how perilously close he comes in his rhetoric to language used by theological liberals, and this language is a result of his defense of inclusivism. Upon reflection, does not an evangelical inclusivist have to acknowledge that *what* people believe (the objective content) is as important as *how* they believe (the subjective intensity)? John Sanders seems to recognize this when he affirms "that some degree of cognitive information is essential for saving faith." Unfortunately, Sanders then retreats in adding "that the Scriptures do not set out the precise amount of information that is required."[20] While we might not all agree on the precise amount of knowledge in view, the information that Scripture does provide far exceeds the requirements of the inclusivists. Most Christians would find the needed information in New Testament texts like John 14:6, Acts 4:12, and Romans 10:9 – 10. But as we will see in chapter 9, inclusivists direct much effort

---

16. Ibid., 158.
17. Ibid.
18. Ibid.
19. For details about that old liberalism, see Ronald Nash, *The New Evangelicalism* (Grand Rapids: Zondervan, 1963).
20. Sanders, *No Other Name*, 229.

toward dismantling the usual evangelical thinking about these texts. Once again it appears that the inclusivist agenda is dictated by a need to disavow anything in Scripture that seems to support exclusivism. For that reason, inclusivists hold a view of faith that is inevitably deficient in theological content.

Even Pinnock relents a bit regarding the objective content to faith. He writes, "This is not to imply the unimportance of making historical facts about Jesus known everywhere. It is essential to make them known in order to clarify God's saving purposes for humanity and to motivate individuals to make their commitment to God in Christ."[21] Inclusivism entails believing that some unevangelized people will nevertheless be saved, but as Pinnock's comment reveals, this does not absolve inclusivists from the duty to practice evangelism. But then, in the next sentence, Pinnock adds that "we cannot reasonably suppose that a failure of evangelization that affects many millions would leave them completely bereft of any access to God."[22]

So the picture is clear: Inclusivists hold that faith can save people even though it is deficient in theological content, yet there is no place in Scripture that asserts this. Indeed, Scripture teaches the precise opposite. While I agree that people are not saved simply by assenting to discrete information, I nevertheless maintain that saving faith has an awareness of such information as one of its necessary conditions (Rom. 10:9 – 10). I believe it is reckless, dangerous, and unbiblical to lead people to think that the preaching of the gospel (which I insist must contain specifics about the person and work of Christ) and personal faith in Jesus are not necessary for salvation. If we do not accept the inclusivist definition of faith, we cannot very well accept the rest of the inclusivist system.

## INCLUSIVISM AND OLD TESTAMENT BELIEVERS

The second plank in the inclusivist system, after the definition of faith, is the distinction between Christians and believers. John Sanders introduces this topic as follows: "If knowledge of Christ is necessary for salvation then how do we explain the sal-

---

21. Pinnock, *A Wideness in God's Mercy*, 159.
22. Ibid.

vation of the Old Testament believers whose knowledge was quite limited concerning the Messiah, but, who yet were justified by faith in God's Word?"[23] Once we accept Sanders's point as a premise, we encounter Clark Pinnock's conclusion: "A person who is informationally premessianic, whether living in ancient or modern times, is in exactly the same spiritual situation."[24] Many Christians find this reasoning persuasive, but I believe an examination will show that they have been too hasty to accept this belief.

The inclusivist argument depends totally on the claim that Old Testament Jewish believers are in precisely the same spiritual situation as present-day non-Christians who nonetheless believe "in God." That expression is in quotation marks because we have to see whether faith as inclusivists define it is directed toward the right object, the true God of Scripture.

The relevant question, I believe, is whether both groups of people really can be regarded the same way. Are there significant differences that might break down the inclusivist's analogy? For one thing, there is the biblical teaching that Old and New Testament believers share a covenantal relationship to God that is grounded on special revelation. The New Testament refers repeatedly to the continuity between Old and New Testament saints (Rom. 1:1 – 2; 11:11 – 24; Gal. 3:8; 6:16; Phil. 3:3, 7, 9; Heb. 11). The Old Testament sacrificial system foreshadowed the one, final sacrifice offered up by Jesus Christ (Heb. 9 – 10). The New Testament reports that the Old Testament saints looked forward to a mediator who would die (John 5:46; 8:56; 1 Peter 1:10 – 12) and how the gospel was preached to Abraham (Gal. 3:6). While there is much about these references that we do not fully understand, we cannot ignore what we see in order to maintain an analogy between Old Testament saints and unevangelized, twentieth-century believers. How can Old Testament believers who had a significant relationship to special revelation and whose faith was tied to symbols and practices that looked forward to Christ provide warrant for treating unevangelized moderns as saved believers? If there is an argument here, I fail to see it.

23. Sanders, "Is Belief in Christ Necessary for Salvation?" 256.
24. Pinnock, *A Wideness in God's Mercy,* 161.

## "HOLY PAGANS"

Inclusivists argue that there is an important Old Testament tradition of "holy pagans." These holy pagans were believing Gentiles who lived outside God's covenant with Israel. They included Melchizedek, Job, the Midian priest Jethro, Naaman, the Roman centurion Cornelius, and even the Magi, who, as Pinnock writes, "came from the East to worship the Christ child and who . . . likely were pagan astrologers (Matthew 2:1 – 12)."[25]

The person in this list who receives the most attention is Melchizedek, whom Pinnock describes as a "pagan" priest who blessed Abram (Gen. 14:19) and whom the New Testament treats as a symbol of Christ's high priestly work (Heb. 7). According to Pinnock, Abram's meeting with Melchizedek in Genesis 14 "makes the point that religious experience may be valid outside Judaism and Christianity."[26] Elsewhere Pinnock suggests that the reason that exclusivists "often refuse to recognize genuine piety outside the church is because they persist in ignoring the scriptural truth symbolized by Melchizedek, and this creates in them a brittleness, rigidity, and narrowness in the presence of non-Christian people."[27]

Once again, let us reflect on this. Even though Genesis identifies Melchizedek as a priest of the most high God, it is not indicated that he is a *pagan*.[28] Melchizedek worshiped and served Yahweh as certainly as Abram did. Melchizedek fails as an example of genuine piety among pagans.

Nor are references to Naaman any more successful. Naaman (2 Kings 5) was clearly a pagan who then confessed his faith in Yahweh (2 Kings 5:15). John Sanders points out that Naaman then requested forgiveness for the times he would enter the temple of the pagan god Rimmon after his return to Syria. Sanders takes this to mean that Naaman continued to have some unorthodox beliefs mixed with his "belief in God."[29]

---

25. Ibid., 95.
26. Ibid., 94.
27. Pinnock, "The Finality of Jesus Christ in a World of Religions," 159.
28. There are some who even hold that Melchizedek was a theophany — a preincarnate appearance of Christ.
29. Sanders, *No Other Name,* 220.

I rather think that Naaman, as an important figure in his society, was occasionally required to participate in civil ceremonies, to his own embarrassment. Either way, nothing in the text suggests that Naaman continued to believe in the pagan deity.

The Magi who sought out the young child Jesus were in all likelihood pagan astrologers. But inclusivists such as Sanders fail to follow up on this and fail to mention that they were in fact seeking Jesus.[30] The example proves nothing.

We have reason to doubt that some in the inclusivists' list of holy pagans (such as Abimelech and Balaam) were saved. Few of the people cited impress us as examples of redeemed believers.

One final line of argument must be noted in this connection. Inclusivists often produce Old Testament texts that mention God's desire to save Gentiles. But these passages are irrelevant to the matter at hand. None of them suggests that these Gentiles could come to experience God's salvation in any way apart from means provided by God in special revelation.

## MORE ON THE DISTINCTION
## BETWEEN CHRISTIANS AND BELIEVERS

The foregoing discussion dealt with the support inclusivists marshal for their distinction between Christians and saved, non-Christian believers. What I find is that inclusivists appeal to a type of faith that is deficient in cognitive content and devoid of any necessary reference to Christ. This kind of faith lacks contact with biblical faith and leads to severely antibiblical consequences. The attempt to link Old Testament believers and possible believers in non-Christian religions collapses entirely because of its inattention to the crucial differences between the two groups.

Attempts to find holy pagans in the Old Testament and then link them to holy pagans in non-Christian religions fails either because the inclusivists' biblical examples were not holy or were no longer pagans. Gentile worshipers of Yahweh in the Old Testament prove by and large to be rather poor role models for the inclusivists' non-Christian believers.

---

30. Ibid., 221.

We can always, of course, engage in long debates about the faith of genuine believers (Jewish and Gentile) during the centuries before Christ. But fishing in those waters hardly yields the results that inclusivists need to support their theory. Coupled with the weaknesses of their appeal to general revelation as a medium of salvation, the theological case for their position looks even less impressive.

## A PIVOTAL INCLUSIVIST ARGUMENT

One of the most important theological arguments for inclusivism is summarized in one sentence by Clark Pinnock: "If God really loves the whole world and desires everyone to be saved, it follows logically that everyone must have access to salvation."[31] How can this seemingly innocuous statement occupy a central place in inclusivist thinking? The answer to the question lies in the second of the two axioms that serve as the foundation for inclusivist thinking. The universality axiom states that God is obliged to give every person a chance to accept or reject his salvation. A loving God must provide every human with access to salvation.

But Pinnock's argument fails for two reasons: (1) It contradicts other elements of his Arminian theology, and (2) it contains a logical fallacy.

## PINNOCK AND THE UNIVERSALITY AXIOM

Theologians familiar with Pinnock's other writings know that he denies God's perfect and complete knowledge of future human actions.[32] If a human being acts as a result of free choice, according to Pinnock, God cannot know about this act before it happens. This means that a great deal of the future is unknowable to God and therefore what theologians call God's omniscience is severely limited in Pinnock's theology. Will the Cleveland Indians ever win another pennant? Pinnock's God

---

31. Pinnock, *A Wideness in God's Mercy,* 157.
32. See Clark H. Pinnock, "Between Classical and Process Theism," in *Process Theology,* ed. Ronald H. Nash (Grand Rapids: Baker, 1987), 309 – 27.

doesn't have a clue. Will some truck driver freely choose to do something dangerous with his vehicle and kill me in the process? Pinnock's God can only wait and see.

But Pinnock's thought does more than limit God's knowledge; it also severely restricts God's power. Reflect a bit on the assumptions at work when we pray. Petitionary prayer is always a request that God exercise his power with regard to certain future states of affairs. But if the future is unknowable to God, it is hard to see what praying can accomplish. How can God know what to do or how to do it if the future is unknown to him? Pinnock's limitation of divine omniscience not only has serious implications for prayer, but also seems inconsistent with the doctrine of providence.

How does this relate to Pinnock's one-sentence argument for the universality axiom? Pinnock announces what God is going to do for every unevangelized person in the world. God *will* (future tense) make access to his salvation available to all. I do not see how Pinnock's God can possibly do that, given his ignorance about the innumerable people and events and relationships involved. We all know how human beings are conceived. Presumably most of those conceptions occur as the result of voluntary human behavior, that is, the kind of future human acts that Pinnock's God cannot know. It would seem to follow that Pinnock's God cannot then know what human beings will exist in the future.

Much of the access that these humans will have to salvation would, it seems, depend upon the voluntary actions of themselves and others. But Pinnock's God must be largely ignorant about all this as well. Once again, we see how ideas have consequences. At this point, Pinnock's theories about God's inability to know future human actions clashes with the universality axiom. Something has to give.

Pinnock's rejection of divine foreknowledge is part of a larger set of beliefs known as Arminianism.[33] As an Arminian,

---

33. The term "Arminian" is derived from the name of Jacob Arminius (1560 – 1609), a Dutch theologian who disputed Calvin's strong stand on predestination. His followers published a five-point remonstrance to what they called the main "errors" in Calvinism. The "Five Points of Calvinism" are the Calvinistic response to these.

Pinnock believes that the salvation of every human being is ultimately up to that person. God can coax and plead with the sinner; the Holy Spirit can do his best; Christ has already died for
the sinner. But the sinner will never experience salvation until
he or she decides to believe. Salvation is a consequence of humans participating with God. God's part was providing a
Savior; the human part involves the use of free will to accept
what God has done. All this is related to why Pinnock and many
other Arminians deny God's perfect knowledge of future human actions; they wrongly think that divine foreknowledge conflicts with human freedom and that this condition conflicts with
the basic premise of their Arminianism.[34]

But let us link together these disparate beliefs of Pinnock.
For the sake of argument, let us assume that (1) God knows absolutely nothing about future human actions that are voluntary,
and (2) the salvation of every individual rests ultimately on that
person's using his or her ability and free will to choose God.
What consequences follow from all this?

For one thing, there is absolutely no way for God *today* to
know that even one person will come to saving faith in the future. More important, there is the realization that while Jesus
was undergoing the agony of the Cross, there was no way God
could know if Christ's atonement would bear fruit in even one
believer. It is ironic how Pinnock's passion for universal accessibility is compatible with a universal rejection of God's offer of
salvation. While God sent his Son to be the Savior of a vast mul-
titude of people, as far as God knew, Jesus could have turned
out to be the Savior of no one!

Theologian J. I. Packer argues that theories like Pinnock's
alter the content of Christian theology so dramatically as to create what Packer calls a new gospel.[35] According to Packer, the
central reference of the *old* gospel was God. Its purpose was "always to give glory to God. It was always and essentially a
proclamation of Divine sovereignty in mercy and judgment, a

---

34. For a discussion of relevant issues, see Ronald Nash, *The Concept of God*
(Grand Rapids: Zondervan, 1983), chap. 4.

35. I should add that Packer says this without making explicit reference to
Pinnock. But there can be no doubt that Pinnock is a proponent of the "new
gospel" that Packer critiques.

summons to bow down and worship the mighty Lord on whom man depends for all good, both in nature and in grace."[36] But the center of reference for the new gospel is not God, but man. The purpose of this new gospel is to help people feel better, not teach them to worship God. The subject of the new gospel is not God's sovereign ways with man, but the help God offers to men.

Packer points out that the advocates of the new gospel

> appeal to men as if they had all the ability to receive Christ at any time; [they] speak of His redeeming work as if He had done no more by dying than make it possible for us to save ourselves by believing; [they] speak of God's love as if it were no more than a general willingness to receive any who will turn and trust; and [they] depict the Father and the Son, not as sovereignly active in drawing sinners to themselves, but as waiting in quiet impotence "at the door of our hearts" for us to let them in.[37]

The old gospel grounds salvation on the work of God while the new gospel makes salvation dependent on a work of man. The old gospel views faith as an integral part of God's gift of salvation while the new gospel sees faith as man's role in salvation. The old gospel gives all the praise to God while the newer one divides the glory between man and God. The new gospel refuses to take sin and human depravity very seriously. Mankind in the new gospel is never so hopeless that we should count someone out in regard to salvation.

The new gospel, Packer continues, "compels us to misunderstand the significance of the gracious invitations of Christ in the gospel . . . [We] now have to read them, not as expressions of the tender patience of a mighty sovereign, but as the pathetic pleadings of an impotent desire; and so the enthroned Lord is suddenly metamorphosed into a weak, futile figure tapping forlornly at the door of the human heart, which He is powerless to open."[38] Packer judges such thinking to be "a shameful dishonour to the Christ of the New Testament."[39] Moreover, the new

---

36. J. I. Packer, "Introductory Essay," in *The Death of Death in the Death of Christ* by John Owen (Edinburgh: Banner of Truth Trust, 1959), 2.

37. Ibid.

38. Ibid., 20.

39. Ibid.

gospel "in effect denies our dependence on God when it comes
to vital decisions, takes us out of His hand, tells us that we are,
after all, what sin taught us to think we were — masters of our
fate, captain of our souls — and so undermines the very foundation of man's religious relationship with His Maker."[40]

Theologian Roger Nicole is troubled by how close the new
gospel comes to resembling the ancient heresy of Pelagianism[41]
by speaking "as if man had a right to come into the presence of
God and enter into account with him, as if God had some oblig-
ation to deal with all people in the same way. The one thing God
owes us is judgment. We ought to marvel at the fact that instead
of confining us all to judgment and damnation, God in his
mercy has been pleased to make plans to save a great multi-
tude."[42]

I began this section by arguing that Pinnock's belief in a
universally accessible salvation clashes logically with his denial
of God's perfect knowledge of the future. It then became necessary to show why — for Pinnock at least — his severe restric-
tions on God's knowledge and power were part of a larger
package of beliefs (Arminianism). Earlier we looked at some
consequences of inclusivist ideas. In this section I have noted
some consequences of Arminianism. There is irony in the way
careless talk about love, compassion, and universal accessibility
can quickly produce shaky theological thinking.

### Pinnock's Fallacy

Even if we ignore Pinnock's eccentric thinking about God's
knowledge and power, there is another problem with his argument: his conclusion does not follow from his premises. Let us
look at the argument in somewhat shortened form: "If an all-loving God desires the salvation of every single human being, then
he will grant every single human being access to salvation."

---

40. Ibid.
41. Pelagianism originated in the early fifth century with certain ideas of a
British monk, Pelagius (d. 418), who carried them to Rome and North Africa.
Pelagius denied original sin and taught that Adam's sin affected only himself.
Hence, human infants are born innocent without any predisposition to sin. This
means that humans have the ability to please God, without any assistance from
God. Obviously, Arminians stop short of Pelagian errors this serious.
42. Roger R. Nicole, "The 'Five Points' and God's Sovereignty," in *Our
Sovereign God*, ed. James M. Boice (Grand Rapids: Baker, 1977), 43.

Even if we grant the truth of the first clause (that God desires the salvation of every human being), does the second follow (that God necessarily will give every human access to that salvation)? Many evangelical Arminians would answer no. As these noninclusivist Arminians see things, God may desire the salvation of all men, *but* getting the gospel (as stated in 1 Corinthians 15:3 – 4) to those people is *our* task. Whether all these noninclusivist Arminians are correct about all the details in their theology is less important right now than the fact that they help us see the flaw in Pinnock's reasoning. God could conceivably desire all kinds of things to happen and still allow those things not to happen for some good reason. Whether or not he chooses to reveal that reason to us, it is still true that the inclusivists' universality axiom does not follow from Pinnock's premises.

## ONE FINAL ARGUMENT

The inclusivists' search for a theological justification for their position involves one more problem. Because of the powerful emotional appeal this final claim has for many people, it may prove to be the inclusivists' most successful argument.

Inclusivists note that almost all Christian exclusivists allow that children who die in infancy as well as people who are mentally incompetent are included within the circle of God's saving grace. I share that belief on the basis of 2 Samuel 12:22 – 23 and other biblical considerations. Inclusivists charge that this belief creates a kind of slippery slope for exclusivists. If babies who die in infancy and mental incompetents will be in heaven without ever coming to explicit faith in Christ, then to be consistent they should grant the same privilege to "innocent" people outside the bounds of Christianity who also die without ever hearing the gospel.[43] If God's salvific will encompasses babies and the mentally incompetent who die unevangelized, why should his saving will not also include all those who have never heard of Christ?

---

43. Sanders, *No Other Name*, 231 – 32.

The question we must ask in evaluating this argument is whether it ignores important differences between infants and mental incompetents on the one hand and unevangelized people on the other hand who are mature enough to be held accountable for their resistance to the light of general revelation. Because there are indeed differences, I fail to see how God's gracious act in the case of infants provides for similar action in the case of mature people who intentionally sin.

Inclusivists also err by suggesting that the only reason people are lost is because they have rejected Christ. But rejecting Jesus is not the only reason that men and women are lost. There are no innocent human beings. Our problems do not result from the fact that we do not know God. They flow from our failure to assent to the light that we have. Bruce Demarest explains the message of Romans 1, "[S]inful man consistently repudiates this elemental knowledge of God [found in general revelation] and perverts it into unspeakable idolatry."[44]

I will acknowledge that there are a number of difficult questions that arise once we admit that babies who die in infancy are saved. Does God save them without their exercising explicit faith in Christ? Does their presence in heaven, not as perpetual infants but as humans grown to maturity, suggest other steps in God's dealing with them after death? I do not know anyone who knows how to answer questions like these, and I see little to be gained by extending speculation beyond what God has chosen to tell us. It does seem fruitless, however, to try to draw inferences from matters we do not know and end up in a great deal of theological speculation that contains the potential for serious harm.

Having dealt with a number of theological issues in this chapter, let us turn next to a new set of issues that we encounter in the inclusivists' appeal to the Bible.

---

44. Demarest, *General Revelation*, 248. As noted in the previous chapter, while general revelation is not sufficient for salvation, it is sufficient for divine judgment.

Chapter Nine

# INCLUSIVISM AND THE BIBLE

Exclusivists and evangelical inclusivists affirm their commitment to the authority of Scripture. One might think that this would make a resolution of their differences rather easy. "Let's sit down," these disagreeing evangelicals might be expected to say, "and just see what the Bible has to say on all this." But we will learn in this chapter just how elusive that hope is. Each side in this dispute is critical of the way people on the other side handle certain key passages of Scripture.

This chapter has two parts. In part 1 we will examine what I judge to be the important texts that inclusivists appeal to in support of their position. We will also discuss exclusivist objections to the inclusivist interpretations of these passages. In part 2 we look at the most important texts that exclusivists appeal to for support and consider the inclusivist response. By the end of the chapter we should have a clear view of the strengths and weaknesses of each position with respect to Scripture.

## SCRIPTURES APPEALED TO
## IN SUPPORT OF INCLUSIVISM

### Acts 10 and the Case of Cornelius

No passage of Scripture is mentioned more often by inclusivists than the story of Cornelius in Acts 10. The context is the period immediately after Pentecost — a hectic time for the early church (Acts 2:41; 4:4). Events were happening fast and furiously, and the threat of persecution was always present (Acts 8:1). It was also a time of some confusion, especially with regard to the relationship between features of the old Judaism and the young church (Acts 11:1 – 3). Was the salvation Christ offered only for Jews? If it was also for Gentiles, was it necessary for those Gentiles to conform to such Jewish rituals as circumcision (Acts 15:1 – 2)? These questions were compounded because the Jewish culture forbad good Jews to eat and fellowship in gentile homes (Gal. 2:11 – 14).

Cornelius was a Roman centurion living in Caesarea. As Acts 10:2 reports, Cornelius "and all his family were devout and God-fearing; he gave generously to those in need and prayed to God regularly." Several matters are worth noting. Luke certainly seems to be telling us that Cornelius, though a Gentile, was a faithful believer in Yahweh. Morally and spiritually he was in precisely the same condition as any faithful and believing Jew of that time who had not yet encountered Jesus. We could go so far as to say that his relationship to Yahweh was similar to that of an Old Testament believer.

That whole first-century community of believers in Yahweh was a kind of transitional generation. Jesus had instituted a new covenant. Hence, it was important for faithful Jews to hear about Jesus as the promised Messiah whose mission, as prophesied in the Old Testament, was to die for human sin and rise again. This is why we find Paul working zealously to bring the message of Christ to his Jewish brothers and sisters. It was also important for gentile believers in Yahweh to hear the same message.

Acts 10 relates the story of how God used Peter to bring Cornelius that message, but the chapter adds an additional piece to the puzzle. Peter was not sure he was acting properly in going to Cornelius. It is clear that he was prejudiced when it came to Gentiles, despite the Great Commission (Matt. 28:19; Acts 1:8). Hence, both Cornelius and Peter had important things to learn. After Peter shared the gospel with Cornelius, the centurion and everyone in his house believed and received the gift of the Holy Spirit.

On the surface it appears that there is nothing in this biblical account to support the inclusivist claim that God saves many unevangelized without any specific reference to Jesus Christ. How did this chapter become so important to the inclusivists' case?

For inclusivists, the key passage in the chapter is verses 34 and 35: "Then Peter began to speak: 'I now realize how true it is that God does not show favoritism but accepts men from every nation who fear him and do what is right.'" These words are cited to show that knowledge of Christ is not necessary for salvation.[1] The entire story is supposed to support the inclusivist distinction between believers and Christians. According to John Sanders, "Cornelius was already a saved believer before Peter arrived but he was not a Christian believer."[2] This bears further examination.

Inclusivists say, on the basis of these verses, that any person who simply fears a supreme being and lives a good life will be accepted by God. That is the inclusivist understanding of what it means to fear God and do what is right, but I disagree. In chapter 8 I took issue with the inclusivists' taking the two points in Hebrews 11:6 (believing that God exists and seeking him) as exhausting the content of saving faith. But their treatment of Acts 10:35 falls to the same error.

Unless we challenge this approach, we will be left with the suggestion that one can approach the Father without the Son, a claim clearly contradicted by John 14:6 and 1 John 2:23. Moreover, the suggestion that living a good life can satisfy God smacks of Pelagianism and again contradicts a major New Testament emphasis. While fearing God and doing what is right are important elements of the Christian commitment, they do not exhaust what it means to be a saved believer. Peter's words in Acts 10:35 complement the oft-cited New Testament emphasis on the centrality of Christ in the salvation process. To use Peter's words to supplant that central point begs the inclusivist question.

None of the inclusivist claims for this chapter stand up when we view Acts 10 in the proper light.[3] Cornelius was a believer in the same sense as every believing Jew prior to Christ. Two conditions prevailed during those transitional years: (1) believing Jews and Gentiles (like Cornelius) needed to know that

---

1. See John Sanders, *No Other Name,* (Grand Rapids: Eerdmans, 1992), 254.
2. Ibid.
3. See F. F. Bruce's helpful analysis of the entire chapter in his commentary *The Book of Acts,* rev. ed. (Grand Rapids: Eerdmans, 1988), 201 – 18.

the Son of God had come into the world and offered his life as a sacrifice for many; and (2) Christian Jews (like Peter) had to learn how to deal with the brewing controversy over Gentiles in the early church.

Clark Pinnock describes Cornelius as "the pagan saint par excellence of the New Testament, a believer in God before he became a Christian."[4] This incredible statement seems to be a desperate attempt to buttress the inclusivist position. Is this Gentile who feared Yahweh and who knew and believed the special revelation God delivered in the Old Testament really a *"pagan* saint"? This key proof-text fails miserably in the case for inclusivism.

## Acts 15

Acts 15 is second only to Acts 10 as a crucial proof-text for inclusivists. John Sanders summarizes what is at stake in this passage:

> Paul argued against the Judaizers that Jesus was Lord and Savior of all and hence that the Gentiles were not to be excluded from God's love. . . . Our situation is somewhat similar to the Council of Jerusalem (Acts 15). At that historic meeting, the leaders of the apostolic church decided to allow Gentiles into the church with less restrictive requirements than had previously been accepted by the Jewish Christians.[5]

The point in this quotation is not entirely clear without its context, but what is behind it is the inclusivist contention that whenever the God of the Bible shows any interest in saving Gentiles, inclusivist assumptions must be present somewhere. We saw this attitude expressed in chapter 8 in reference to Old Testament passages that promise the salvation of Gentiles. As I explained, these Old Testament passages do nothing of the kind.

The question now is whether the debate at the Council of Jerusalem has implications for inclusivism. I believe it does not. Paul was arguing that the Christian church can and should include believing Gentiles without their having to conform to

---

4. Clark Pinnock, *A Wideness in God's Mercy* (Grand Rapids: Zondervan, 1992), 165.

5. Sanders, *No Other Name,* 137.

traditional Jewish practices such as circumcision. But these Gentiles were to become believers through explicit faith in the finished work of Jesus Christ. How this passage can support the belief that millions of Gentiles can be saved apart from faith in Christ is left unexplained by inclusivists.

### Acts 14:16 – 17

Speaking to a crowd in the city of Lystra, Paul and Silas explained, "In the past, [God] let all nations go their own way. Yet he has not left himself without testimony: He has shown kindness by giving you rain from heaven and crops in their seasons; he provides you with plenty of food and fills your hearts with joy." According to Pinnock, this verse indicates that God had a witness or testimony among people who had not heard the gospel. Apparently, Pinnock declares, "these people possessed truth from God in the context of their [pagan] religion and culture."[6] I disagree, because Acts 14:16 does not teach that other nations were saved, only that God continued to have an ongoing witness among them through general revelation. Absolutely nothing in Paul's words suggests that the Lystrans received God's witness through their pagan faith or that the witness they received through general revelation was sufficient to effect their salvation.

### Acts 17:28 – 30

Acts 17 contains Paul's memorable message to Athenian intellectuals, in which he quotes from a pagan Stoic philosopher: "'For in him we live and move have our being.' As some of your own poets have said, 'We are his offspring'"(v. 28). Pinnock regards Paul's action as an endorsement of pagan religious sentiments.[7]

Alan Race claims that Paul's message "acknowledges the authenticity of the worship of the men of Athens at their altar 'to an unknown God.'"[8] Race's claim, however, is falsified, first, by

6. Clark Pinnock, "The Finality of Jesus Christ in a World of Religions," in *Christian Faith and Practice in the Modern World*, ed. Mark A. Noll and David F. Wells (Grand Rapids: Eerdmans, 1988), 158.

7. Pinnock, *A Wideness in God's Mercy*, 96.

8. Alan Race, *Christians and Religious Pluralism* (Maryknoll, N.Y.: Orbis Books, 1982), 39.

the conclusion to Paul's sermon: "For [God] has set a day when he will judge the world with justice by the man he has appointed. He has given proof of this to all men by raising him from the dead" (v. 31). It is falsified in the second place in that Paul's words led some in the audience to turn from their false gods to the truth (v. 34). Pinnock seems to forget that Paul was an educated man addressing an audience of educated people. What better way to gain their attention than to show that he was acquainted with some of their writers and could quote them? One quote hardly proves that Paul had any interest in or sympathy with Stoic thought.[9]

Pinnock has more to say on this text. In verse 30, Paul states, "In the past God overlooked such ignorance, but now he commands all people everywhere to repent." For Pinnock, these words teach that God overlooks the sins of all who fail to trust in him because of ignorance. New Testament scholar F. F. Bruce has a better grasp of Paul's meaning: However patient God may have been prior to the coming of Christ, Paul is saying that the time of patience has ended. Bruce states, "If ignorance of the divine nature was culpable before [Christ's coming], it is inexcusable now. Let all people everywhere (the Athenians included) repent therefore of their false conception of God (and consequent flouting of his will) and embrace the true knowledge of his being now made available in the gospel."[10]

It is difficult to see how passages that clearly call upon lost pagans to place their faith in Christ can be treated as proof-texts for the inclusivist position that saving faith can exist apart from Christ.

## Texts Cited for Universal Accessibility of Salvation

There is a considerable number of Scripture texts that inclusivists quote frequently in support of the universality axiom. This axiom, we remember, is one of two fundamental axioms of the inclusivist system and states that God is obliged to make his salvation accessible to every person throughout world history. It is this axiom that distinguishes inclusivists from exclusivists,

---

9. For more on this, see Ronald Nash, *The Gospel and the Greeks* (Dallas: Probe Books, 1992).

10. Bruce, *The Book of Acts*, 340.

because both groups agree on the other one — the particularity axiom, which asserts that Jesus is the only Savior.

The biblical texts appealed to in support of universally accessible salvation are familiar and include the following:

> God our Savior . . . wants all men to be saved and to come to a knowledge of the truth (1 Tim. 2:3 – 4).

> For the grace of God that brings salvation has appeared to all men (Titus 2:11).

> [God] is patient with you, not wanting anyone to perish, but everyone to come to repentance (2 Peter 3:9).

> He is the atoning sacrifice for our sins, and not only for ours but also for the sins of the whole world (1 John 2:2).

The one feature common to these and other supposed universalist texts is their use of words such as "all" and "world," which inclusivists insist must always mean every human person. But it is not at all clear that these texts teach what inclusivists claim they teach. Consider Titus 2:11. Does the expression "all men" really refer to every single human being who has ever lived or will live? How can it?

Many theologians point out that expressions like "all men" may refer either to all humans *without distinction* or to all persons *without exception*. In their view, texts such as Titus 2:11 do not describe what God has done or is doing for all humans without exception, that is, for every single human being; rather, they report what God did for all human beings without distinction. That is, Christ did not die just for Jews or for males or for educated people or for powerful individuals. He also died for Gentiles, for women and children, for barbarians, for slaves and the poor. He died for Jews, yes; but he also died for Romans, Thracians, Syrians, Ethiopians, Macedonians, and Samaritans. All these passages — 1 Timothy 2:3 – 4, Titus 2:11, 2 Peter 3:9, and 1 John 2:2 — tell us what God has done for all humans without distinction.[11]

---

11. I recognize how this last claim only scratches the surface of this problem, but it is impractical to pursue the matter further in this book. I recommend a classic work on the subject, *The Death of Death in the Death of Christ* by John Owen (Edinburgh: Banner of Truth Trust, 1959). Owen, a Puritan scholar, provides a detailed analysis of "every" universalist text.

*Summary*

So far we have examined the biblical passages most often appealed to by inclusivists, and to my mind this has left their biblical support very weak. Coupled with the theological weaknesses identified in chapter 8, this discussion should lead many people sympathetic to inclusivism to re-examine their commitment.

## SCRIPTURES APPEALED TO
## IN SUPPORT OF EXCLUSIVISM

It seems evident that, on the surface at least, exclusivism is on much firmer ground biblically than inclusivism. Not only is there a host of well-known Bible texts that teach the precise opposite of inclusivism, but also the whole thrust of New Testament evangelism and missions seems to run contrary to inclusivist assumptions. To close out this chapter I will cite a number of these exclusivist passages and then consider the inclusivist response.

### Romans 10:9 – 10

> That if you confess with your mouth, "Jesus is Lord," and believe in your heart that God raised him from the dead, you will be saved. For it is with your heart that you believe and are justified, and it is with your mouth that you confess and are saved.

John Sanders says of this text, "It is clear from Romans 10:9 that whoever confesses Jesus as Lord and believes in his heart that God raised him from the dead will be saved. It is not clear that whoever does not fulfill these conditions is lost. Paul simply does not specify how much a person has to know to be saved."[12]

Sanders regards this passage as a conditional statement comparable to "If it rains, then the sidewalk will get wet." That is, if you confess Jesus as Lord and believe in your heart that God raised him, you will be saved. Both conditional statements

---

12. Sanders, *No Other Name*, 67.

are true, Sanders assures us. But turning the nonbiblical sentence around does not yield a true proposition. The sidewalk could be wet even though it has not rained. The sidewalk might have gotten wet some other way — from a sprinkling system, for example.

Similarly, Sanders insists, we are not entitled to turn around the conditional statement in Romans 10:9 – 10. In Sanders's words, "It is sometimes argued that since all those who accept Christ are saved, it must follow that *only* those who know about and accept Christ are saved. But this is like arguing that since all Collies are dogs, all dogs must be Collies."[13] Sanders's logic is acceptable in the case of the relationships *rain/wet sidewalk* and *Collies/dogs*. The conditional reasoning in these cases works in one direction but fails when reversed. Is Sanders, then, correct when he states that "All who receive Christ will be saved" is not synonymous with "All who do not receive Christ will be lost"?[14]

If Sanders is right, the traditional exclusivist meaning applied to Romans 10:9 – 10 turns out to be an embarrassing logical blunder.

Sanders is right about one thing: Propositions of the form *If A, then B* do not convert simply to *If B, then A*. Likewise, propositions of the form *All A is B* do not convert to *All B is A*. However, there is one exception to this general rule: *All A is B* does convert to *All B is A* whenever *A* and *B* are identical. If the class of all people who have saving faith in Jesus Christ (call this *A*) is identical with the class of all saved believers (call this *B*), then every member of *A* is also a member of *B* and vice versa. In such a case, one is entitled to say both that *All A is B* and that *All B is A*. The same situation affects hypothetical statements like *If A, then B*.

This detour into logic reveals that the inclusivist argument cannot be used to disqualify Romans 10:9 – 10 because that would beg the very question we are attempting to settle. What Sanders does instead is simply assume that the two classes of people are different (which is tantamount to assuming his inclusivism) and then use that assumption to alter the meaning of the

13. John Sanders, "Is Belief in Christ Necessary for Salvation?" *Evangelical Quarterly* 60 (1988): 246 – 47.
14. Ibid., 248.

text. Unfortunately, Sanders does not allow at all that the exclusivist interpretation of Romans 10:9 – 10 is a *possible* reading of the text.

### Acts 4:12

At first glance the meaning of this text seems clear: "Salvation is found in no one else, for there is no other name under heaven given to men by which we must be saved." But the inclusivists marshal this verse for support by a procedure that proves to be quite revealing.

According to Clark Pinnock, Acts 4:12 does not speak in any way to the "fate of unevangelized people, whether they lived before or after Christ."[15] Pinnock states further that "The text speaks forcefully about the incomparable power of Jesus' name to save (and heal) those who hear and respond to the good news, but it does not comment on the fate of the heathen."[16] For Pinnock, this verse "does not render a judgment, positive or negative, on another question that interests us a great deal: the status of other religions and the role they play in God's providence or plan of redemption."[17] But this runs counter to the verse's unequivocal statement that "salvation is found in no one else."

Pinnock does here essentially what John Sanders does with Romans 10:9 – 10. Pinnock agrees that Jesus is doing something unique and wonderful for the world, but he denies that this is necessarily God's exclusive way.[18] Further, he states,

> Acts 4:12 makes a strong and definitively exclusive claim about the messianic, holistic salvation Jesus has brought into the world. It is a salvation that is incomparable and without rival. It is available through no other name than Jesus the Incarnate Son of God. But the text does not exclude from eternal salvation the vast majority of people who have ever lived on the earth.[19]

---

15. Clark Pinnock, "Acts 4:12 — No Other Name Under Heaven," in *Through No Fault of Their Own?* ed. William V. Crockett and James G. Sigountos (Grand Rapids: Baker, 1991), 110.

16. Ibid.

17. Ibid.

18. See ibid., 112.

19. Ibid., 115.

Responding to this view, Darrell Bock, an exclusivist who teaches at Dallas Theological Seminary, concurs with Pinnock that the text emphasizes a holistic salvation that includes both physical and spiritual healing. Bock also acknowledges that the text does not speak *directly* to the issue of exclusivism. Nonetheless, he contends that Pinnock attaches too much significance to ideas the text does not express. Alluding to references to the "God-fearing Greeks" and spiritual "ignorance" mentioned elsewhere by Paul, Bock writes that "respect for those who seek God is not the same as acceptance of their faith as 'true' or 'saving.' Luke knows the difference. Acts 4:12 is not 'unfairly manipulated' by exclusivists; rather it is related properly by them to the assertions and implications of the speeches in Acts 13 and 17."[20]

Bock correctly points out the importance of relating Peter's words in Acts 4:12 to a broader context, namely, the messages found in Acts 13 and 17. But if receiving light from two additional chapters of Acts is good, then consulting the entire book of Acts is even better. What I learned as a result of this exercise contributes to the conclusion of this book.

### John 14:6

In this familiar passage Jesus declares, "I am the way and the truth and the life. No one comes to the Father except through me." John Sanders feels that this verse says nothing about the unevangelized. Rather, while it states that all who believe in Christ will be saved, it does not mean to say that all who fail to believe in him will be lost.[21] I disagree.

There is an epistemological component present in the words *way, truth,* and *life.*[22] The inclusivist position effectively negates

---

20. Darrell L. Bock, "Athenians Who Have Never Heard," in *Through No Fault of Their Own?* 124.

21. Sanders, *No Other Name,* 64.

22. I am referring to the inclusivists' distinction between the ontological and epistemological necessity of Christ's redemptive work as it was discussed in chapter 7. Inclusivists maintain that everyone who receives God's salvation does so only on the basis of Christ's redemption (the ontological dimension), but that actually *knowing* (the epistemological dimension) about that work is not necessary.

Jesus' use of these words by denying the epistemological necessity of Christ's redemptive work. What good is a way and a
truth and a life that people know nothing about? The words "No
one comes to the Father except through me" are hardly compatible with inclusivist sentiments.

## Other Texts

There are several other exclusivist texts that I believe speak
for themselves:

> Yet to all who received him, to those who believed in his
> name, he gave the right to become children of God (John
> 1:12).

> For God so loved the world that he gave his one and only
> Son, that whoever believes in him shall not perish but have
> eternal life. . . . Whoever believes in him is not condemned,
> but whoever does not believe stands condemned already be-
> cause he has not believed in the name of God's one and only
> Son (John 3:16, 18).

> No one who denies the Son has the Father; whoever ac-
> knowledges the Son has the Father also (1 John 2:23).

> He who has the Son has life; he who does not have the
> Son of God does not have life (1 John 5:12).

I submit that between words like these and the words of inclusivists there is a world of difference. I believe I have shown
that the inclusivist support from Scripture stands on shaky
ground and reflects a tendency to explain away clear biblical
statements that run contrary to their view.

Chapter Ten

# SOME REMAINING QUESTIONS

Several important questions related to inclusivism remain to be discussed. I begin with a question about Clark Pinnock.

## IS PINNOCK REALLY AN INCLUSIVIST?

To see the point here, let us recall that an inclusivist is someone who believes that while Christ's redemptive work is ontologically necessary for salvation, it is not epistemologically necessary. This means that if anyone in any religious system is saved, it will be because of the redemptive work of Jesus Christ. But receiving God's salvation does not depend upon knowing about Jesus or believing in him.

While Pinnock claims to be an inclusivist, he is also known for his defense of a theory that is logically incompatible with inclusivism. Pinnock supports a position known as "post-mortem evangelism." This is the view that everyone who has not had a chance to hear the gospel in this life (before physical death) will be presented with the gospel *after* death.[1]

---

1. John Sanders discusses Pinnock's position in *No Other Name* (Grand Rapids: Eerdmans, 1992), 261–64. The theory can be found in early chapters of Pinnock's book *A Wideness in God's Mercy* (Grand Rapids: Zondervan, 1992) and in an unpublished paper, "Inclusive Finality or Universally Accessible Salvation," presented at the 1989 annual meeting of the Evangelical Theological Society. Pinnock speaks clearly in an article about "The hope of an opportunity to accept Christ's salvation after death, only hinted at in 1 Peter 4:6 but based on the reasonable assumption that God would not reject the perishing sinners whom he loves without ever knowing what their response to his grace would be" ("Toward an Evangelical Theology of Religions," *Journal of the Evangelical Theological Society* 33 [1990]: 368). Note that Pinnock believes that God, with his severely limited knowledge of the future, can never know what people's future response to his grace will be.

Generally speaking, people who teach post-mortem evangelism (or P.M.E. for brevity's sake) are not really inclusivists. They
are actually exclusivists who believe that a conscious act of faith
in Jesus Christ really is necessary for salvation. The reason that
they teach that humans have a chance at salvation after death is
obvious. If God is going to save people who have not heard the
gospel in this life and if explicit faith in Jesus Christ is necessary
for salvation, then only one conclusion is possible:[2] The unevangelized must have an opportunity to hear the gospel after death.

The reason that the doctrine of P.M.E. is inconsistent with
inclusivism should be apparent. Inclusivists teach that explicit
faith in Jesus Christ is not necessary for salvation; advocates of
P.M.E. believe that it is. Inclusivists hold that general revelation
can bring people to salvation; advocates of P.M.E. do not.[3]

How can Pinnock hope to present himself as both an inclusivist and an exclusivist who believes in P.M.E.?[4] Is he really an
inconsistent exclusivist, perhaps? Or is he a confused inclusivist? Or is he indifferent to this issue because he "knows" that
God will save millions of people who have never heard the
gospel. But as we saw in chapter 9, not even *God* can know this,
according to Pinnock. Does Pinnock, then, know something that
God cannot know? Is he simply guessing or hoping? Something
seems amiss in all this.

## WHAT ABOUT SALVATION AFTER DEATH?

We would hope that eventually Pinnock will dispel the confusion, but in the meantime we should look at post-mortem
evangelism, the theory that helps to create the uncertainty. Does

---

2. As John Sanders explains in part 3 of *No Other Name,* there are some other
options. For example, some believe that God will find a way to get his message
to everyone before death (as through dreams, perhaps) or that God reaches
everyone with a chance to believe the gospel at the moment of death. But such
thinking also contradicts inclusivism by teaching the necessity of faith in Christ
and breaks with the doctrine of P.M.E. by teaching that salvation must occur before death. Sanders's discussion of these matters is helpful.

3. Sanders admits this on page 189 of *No Other Name.*

4. For the record, Pinnock has never admitted that his advocacy of P.M.E. is a
variant of exclusivism.

the doctrine of P.M.E. make sense theologically? Does it have support from Scripture?

John Sanders[5] locates the theory of P.M.E. in nonevangelicals such as Joseph Leckie[6] and Yale Professor George Lindbeck,[7] but he also finds the view defended by more evangelical thinkers such as Gabriel Fackre,[8] Donald Bloesch,[9] John Lawson,[10] and Wayne Grudem.[11] The position is widely taught in Southern Baptist colleges and seminaries.

Evangelicals who teach post-mortem salvation see the theory supported by three other beliefs: (1) No one will be saved apart from conscious knowledge of and explicit faith in Jesus; (2) the reason that any person is lost is his or her conscious rejection of Christ; and (3) God makes salvation accessible to all human beings. Note that anyone who accepts these three claims must reject the inclusivist's confidence in the salvific efficacy of general revelation. Even those who believe that general revelation provides enough knowledge to save admit that it does not include any information about Jesus' redemptive work. Because advocates of P.M.E. insist that conscious faith in Jesus is necessary for salvation, it seems best to view these people as exclusivists rather than inclusivists. And since it is obvious that the universal accessibility of salvation (proposition 3) does not occur within the lifetimes of large numbers of people, the information about the gospel that is necessary for salvation can only come after death.

Defenders of post-mortem salvation deny that they are teaching a doctrine of a "second chance" because, they argue, the people who hear the gospel after death are those who never

---

5. Sanders, *No Other Name*, chap. 6.

6. Joseph Leckie, *The World to Come and Final Destiny*, 2d ed. (Edinburgh: T. & T. Clark, 1922).

7. George Lindbeck, *The Nature of Doctrine: Religion and Theology in a Postliberal Age* (Philadelphia: Westminster, 1984).

8. Gabriel Fackre, *The Christian Story: A Narrative Interpretation of Basic Christian Doctrine*, rev. ed. (Grand Rapids: Eerdmans, 1984).

9. Donald Bloesch, *Essentials of Evangelical Theology* (San Francisco: Harper & Row, 1978).

10. John Lawson, *Introduction to Christian Doctrine* (Wilmore, Ky.: Francis Asbury Press, 1980).

11. Wayne Grudem, "Christ Preaching Through Noah: 1 Peter 3:19 – 20 in the Light of Dominant Themes in Jewish Literature," *Trinity Journal* 7 (1986): 4.

had a *first* chance. Hence, this view must be distinguished from
a form of universalism that teaches that *all* humans, including
those who have rejected the gospel in this life, will have a second chance after death. Indeed, most of the proponents of this
latter view believe that God will grant the unrepentant a third
chance and a fourth chance and so on, until finally God's love
triumphs over all human recalcitrance.[12]

One theological reason often given for supporting P.M.E. is
that it provides a helpful way of understanding the salvation of
dead infants and mental incompetents. Advocates of P.M.E. ask
whether people who die in infancy are really saved without explicit faith in Christ. Would it not solve a lot of problems to say
that they are given a chance to accept Christ after death? Of
course, this approach would raise the possibility that many dead
infants and mental incompetents might reject Christ after death.

It seems best to reserve judgment on this matter until we
see how plausible the case for P.M.E. is. The appeal to the case of
dead infants, after all, is not really an argument. It simply points
to one possible benefit from accepting a belief in salvation after
death.

The obvious question then becomes, What does Scripture
teach about the subject? Advocates of P.M.E. appeal to five major texts: 1 Peter 3:18 – 4:6; Acts 17:31; 2 Timothy 4:8; 1 John 4:17;
and John 5:25 – 29. I believe that the last four of these texts really
do not speak at all to the subject, and we need not discuss them
here. However, I encourage readers to study them. But the long
passage in 1 Peter is quite a different matter. First Peter 3:18 – 21
states the following:

> For Christ died for sins once for all, the righteous for the un-
> righteous, to bring you to God. He was put to death in the
> body but made alive by the Spirit, through whom also he
> went and preached to the spirits in prison who disobeyed
> long ago when God waited patiently in the days of Noah

---

12. This last paragraph may require some qualification since some, like Clark
Pinnock, believe there is uncertainty about what constitutes a genuine and fair
opportunity to accept the gospel. Did the Christian evangelist do a good job, or
was he having a bad day? Was the person who rejected the gospel distracted?
All this suggests that Pinnock may be defending a modified form of the Second
Chance doctrine.

while the ark was being built. In it only a few people, eight in
all, were saved through water, and this water symbolizes bap-
tism that now saves you also — not the removal of dirt from
the body but the pledge of a good conscience toward God.

In the verses that follow this passage, Peter talks about how
Christians reject the wicked lifestyle of the unsaved. Because of
this rejection, Christians suffer abuse from the unsaved, who
one day will stand before the Judge of the living and the dead.
Then Peter writes, "For this is the reason the gospel was
preached even to those who are now dead, so that they might be
judged according to men in regard to the body, but live according to God in regard to the spirit" (1 Peter 4:6).

It is customary for advocates of P.M.E. to link 1 Peter 4:6
with the reference to Noah's ark and "the spirits in prison." They
view the latter as an allusion to Christ's descent into hell (a concept that is also debated among evangelicals). But such a tactic is
very weak exegetically; it fails to recognize that 1 Peter 4:1 – 5
slips totally alien subject matter into the middle of what P.M.E.
supporters treat as one unbroken line of thought. I believe this
exegesis is faulty, because we are left to ask what these five
verses are doing in the middle of a discussion on a different subject. Those five verses make it extremely unlikely that 1 Peter 4:6
and its reference to preaching to those now dead are somehow
connected with the immediately preceding passage, 3:18 – 21.

First Peter 4:6 may well be a reference to the common biblical practice of describing Christians as people who are now
"dead" to — that is, oblivious to — certain things in their past.
In Galatians 2:20 Paul describes himself as "crucified with Christ
and I no longer live, but Christ lives in me." In Romans 6:2, Paul
states that Christians have died to sin. Peter may well be saying
something similar in 1 Peter 4:6. Of course, it is also possible that
Peter is only telling us at this early stage in the life of the church
that many to whom the gospel came have since died physically,
even though they are still alive and conscious in the spirit.

My point is that the post-mortem salvation reading of 1
Peter 4:6 is neither the only nor the most plausible interpretation. Wise Christians never base an important doctrine, especially one that is controversial, on a single, highly debatable

passage of Scripture. If this approach were applied by P.M.E. advocates to 1 Corinthians 15:29, it would result in Christians being urged to follow a policy of baptizing living people as proxies for the unbaptized dead. It is clear, then, that there are many reasons not to think that 1 Peter 4:6 teaches that humans will have opportunity to hear the gospel after death.

What about 1 Peter 3:19 – 20, which states that through the Spirit Christ also "went and preached to the spirits in prison who disobeyed long ago when God waited patiently in the days of Noah"? What does this mean? This verse is often injected into the debate over P.M.E. because they understand it to say that between his death and resurrection, Jesus descended into the lower world and evangelized some group of people already dead. The reason this view does not work is that verse 20 appears to describe the recipients of Christ's message as unbelievers who lived during the time of Noah. Did Jesus preach to these unbelievers back before the Flood? But why would he preach only to unbelievers in that situation? Why did he not also preach to the believing Patriarchs of the Old Testament who could have profited from what Jesus had to say? Why did he preach only *before* the Flood? All these questions suggest that the interpretation under consideration is badly off track.

There is a good reason why 1 Peter 3 *cannot* teach any kind of post-mortem evangelism. The context finds Peter urging Christians to continue faithful in their evangelism and witnessing in spite of persecution. It would make no sense for Peter to say this and at the same time tell the persecuted Christians that the unbelievers behind all their suffering will have a second chance to be saved after they die. Sanders responds that Peter's words are designed not to encourage Christians to worldly living.[13] But I think Sanders misses the point. Why would Peter urge Christians to persist in their witness to Christ if these same unbelievers will be given a chance to be saved after they die? If Peter intended to acknowledge P.M.E. anywhere in this book, this would be the place to do so. The fact that Peter does not

---

13. In other words, Sanders suggests, if Peter's readers really came to believe that their ungodly tormentors would be saved after death, this would incline them to worldliness. See Sanders, *No Other Name,* 207 – 8.

strongly suggests that post-mortem evangelism was not relevant to his message.

What, then, was Peter talking about? Some understand 1 Peter 3 to say that Christ preached to the lost while he was alive and that those lost people were figuratively in prison; and that Christ's preaching to the lost was analogous to Noah's preaching to the lost before the Flood. Still another interpretation suggests that 1 Peter 3:19 speaks of how the Spirit of Christ (1 Peter 1:11) spoke through Noah (2 Peter 2:5) to men and women who are now in a prison of judgment. They were judged for their disobedience and are suffering the consequences. Through Noah's preaching, they were exposed to the light and rejected it. In neither of these more plausible interpretations is there the slightest indication of any later chance at salvation.

Several other issues remain. First, advocates of P.M.E. believe that the reason people are lost is that they reject Christ. Once this is assumed, it seems to follow that unevangelized people who have never had a chance to reject or accept Christ must be given that opportunity after death. But the assumption is false. The reason why people are lost is clearly described in Romans 3: "There is no one righteous, not even one.... All have sinned and fall short of the glory of God" (vv. 10, 23). Rejecting Christ is not a condition for being lost. We are lost already (Ps. 51:5; Eph. 2:1 – 3).

Second, according to Pinnock, the decisions that beneficiaries of post-mortem evangelism make after death will reflect the direction they were heading during their lives. Sanders seems to agree, explaining that "those who exercised the faith principle in life will continue in faith and love Christ, while those who rejected God's revelation and mercy in life will continue to resist and hate God. In other words, people will tend to be confirmed in the direction they were already heading."[14] However, there may be surprising exceptions, Sanders continues, in that people who hated God in this life may choose to believe after post-mortem evangelization.

My question is, Is there any basis in Scripture for this kind of speculation? I am disturbed that the inclusivists we have cited

14. Sanders, *No Other Name*, 262.

in this book engage in sheer speculation and then use their con-
jectures as the basis for conclusions that have enormous consequences for Christian faith and practice. I will return to this
point in the next chapter.

It is also worth noting that Pinnock believes that the fate of
the evangelized (that is, Christian believers) *may* be fixed at
death.[15] If that were not so, we could end up with a theology in
which unbelievers in this life end up saved *and* believers in this
life end up lost!

Third, I am concerned as to which of the two positions we
are considering must bear the burden of proof. I believe that
quite obviously the burden of proof falls upon the shoulders of
those who contend that there can be salvation after death. In the
last chapter I invite readers to search through the book of Acts
for any sign of inclusivist convictions among the early
Christians. I believe the search is futile, equally so if we were
seeking indications of a commitment to post-mortem evangelism.

While the early Christian writing known as 2 Clement is not
part of the New Testament, it nonetheless reflects the thinking of
Christians during the church's first century. Second Clement 8:3
states that "after we have gone out of the world, no further
power of confessing or repenting will there belong to us." It is
possible that this assertion became necessary because some, as
the first century drew to a close, may have raised the possibility
of salvation after death. I suggest also that comments as clear as
Second Clement 8:3 do not appear in the New Testament because they simply were not needed among the members of a
community whose every action recognized that physical death
marked the boundary of human salvific opportunity.

If I insist that the burden of proof rests on the advocates of
P.M.E., it is because they must overcome the clear implication of
numerous New Testament passages that teach that God's judgment will be based on events, deeds, and commitments occurring in this life. Matthew 7:13 – 23 comes to mind in this
connection. In verses 13 – 14 Jesus warns his listeners of the
broad road and wide gate that lead to destruction, and he urges

---

15. See Sanders's discussion on the same page.

them to be among the few that enter the narrow gate and follow the narrow road that leads to life. There is no place for a salvific opportunity after death in these words.

Jesus issues a warning about false prophets who come in sheep's clothing (Matt. 7:15 – 20) and concludes by saying, "Every tree that does not bear good fruit is cut down and thrown into the fire." The emphasis is, once again, upon what occurs during an earthly lifetime.

In Matthew 7:21 – 23 Jesus speaks of those who will come to him at the judgment saying, "Lord, Lord, did we not prophesy in your name, and in your name drive out demons and perform many miracles?" In response, Jesus reports that he will tell them plainly, "I never knew you. Away from me, you evildoers!" Once again, post-mortem judgment is based upon pre-mortem conditions. The point likewise appears in Matthew 7:24 – 27, Jesus' well-known story of the men who built their respective houses on rock and sand.

We do well also to study Jesus' parables in Matthew 13. Explaining the parable of the weeds (vs. 24 – 30, 36 – 43), Jesus states, "As the weeds are pulled up and burned in the fire, so it will be at the end of the age. The Son of Man will send out his angels, and they will weed out of his kingdom everything that causes sin and all who do evil." The sin and evil referred to here must pertain to things done prior to one's death. There are no qualifications in this or other passages; there are no hints of exceptions arising from events after death. A similar point appears in Matthew 24:41 – 46.

In Revelation 20:11 – 15, John records a vision of the judgment before the Great White Throne, when the books were to be opened and "The dead were judged according to what they had done as recorded in the books" (v. 12). Again, the clear message is that judgment has our human lives on earth in view.

In all these passages and more, I contend, one simple point stands out and is taken for granted: Physical death marks the boundary of human opportunity. Anyone who wishes to argue that Jesus and the authors of the New Testament believed otherwise must shoulder the burden of proof. Given the serious implications of a belief in post-mortem salvation for evangelism and missions, the total silence of Scripture regarding opportunities after death should trouble advocates of P.M.E. The highly suspect theological arguments offered in support of the position have already been examined in this chapter and have been found to be broken reeds, unable to support the weight of the theory. We noted, for example, that it simply is not true that humans are lost solely because they have rejected Christ. In an earlier chapter we discussed the doctrine of the universal accessibility of salvation, a necessary presupposition for those holding to post-mortem salvation. For the record, some evangelical inclusivists such as John Sanders reject the doctrine.[16]

By way of conclusion let me cite Hebrews 9:27: "man is destined to die once, and after that to face judgment." Many proponents of P.M.E. claim that this verse is the only New Testament text that even comes close to declaring death as the boundary of human opportunity.[17] Such a claim is simplistic, once we recognize the extent to which the many New Testament passages about divine judgment presuppose this fact. Nothing in Hebrews 9:27 teaches that a person's judgment follows immediately upon his death. Rather, the verse gives the order as death first and judgment second. The judgment comes after death, but nothing is said about how long after death it occurs. Once that is settled, it is clear that the intent of the verse is to show that the judgment of each human reflects that person's standing with God at the moment of death.

## WHAT ABOUT OTHER RELIGIONS?

Many Christians will have no difficulty recognizing some elements of truth in non-Christian religions even though they may find the central beliefs of each system to be incompatible

---

16. Ibid., 210. Sanders's major reason for rejecting P.M.E. is the fact that the doctrine assumes that conscious belief in Jesus Christ is necessary for salvation. Unlike Clark Pinnock, Sanders recognizes that this assumption is logically incompatible with his inclusivism.

17. I am intentionally passing over Jesus' parable of Lazarus and the rich man in Luke 16:19 – 31. Interpretations of the parable get mired in endless debates because it is a parable. I personally believe that the passage provides important information about the afterlife and the fact that death seals human destiny, but as a realist I recognize that such a parable is difficult to use to prove a point about P.M.E.

with revealed truth. Bruce Demarest explains that the Christian conviction that Christ is the only Savior

> does not deny that good exists in other religions, or that the non-Christian faiths do not embody valid spiritual insights. On the basis of universal general revelation rendered meaningful by common grace, the non-Christian religions . . . possess elements of truth about God and man. But Jesus Christ, the eternal Son of God, fulfills and transcends the valid insights possessed by all the non-Christian systems.[18]

Demarest rejects thinking that sees only errors and lies in non-Christian religions. "On the basis of God's universal general revelation and common enabling grace," he continues,

> undisputed truths about God, man, and sin lie embedded to varying degrees in the non-Christian religions. In addition to elements of truth, the great religions of the world frequently display a sensitivity to the spiritual dimension of life, a persistence in devotion, a readiness to sacrifice, and sundry virtues both personal (gentleness, serenity of temper) and social (concern for the poor, nonviolence). But in spite of these positive features, natural man, operating within the context of natural religion and lacking special revelation, possesses a fundamentally false understanding of spiritual truth.[19]

Demarest concludes, "The world's non-Christian religions, then, are essentially false, but with glimpses of truth afforded by general revelation. It needs to be emphasized that the light they do possess is too fragmentary and distorted to illumine the path that leads to a saving knowledge of God."[20]

Paul used moments of truth in the thinking of his pagan audience on Mars Hill as points of personal and cultural contact during his evangelistic message (Acts 17). We can and often should do the same in our dealings with people from other religions. But this hardly means that such people are already saved or will be saved in the future because of the non-Christian

---

18. Bruce A. Demarest, *General Revelation* (Grand Rapids: Zondervan, 1982), 254.

19. Ibid., 259.

20. Ibid.

beliefs. Paul did not tell the Athenians that the unknown God they worshiped could save; rather, he told them about the only true God and his Son, the only Savior. None of those who continued to follow their old convictions were saved, while those who believed Paul were saved (Acts 17:34).

## WHAT ABOUT HELL?

The topic of hell has been in the background throughout this book. Both pluralists and inclusivists use the doctrine for emotional appeal in the debate over exclusivism,[21] and sometimes this is exploited. Regrettably, critics of exclusivism do not always play fair; they ignore important differences among exclusivists, cite only the extreme positions, and rely on misrepresentations and distortions.

A typical distortion is the charge that in the exclusivist view, God gives large numbers of the human race absolutely no chance to be saved and therefore those same unfortunate souls will spend eternity being tortured by a vengeful God. Some, for example, speak of "a cruel God serving as a sort of proprietor of hell" and of a "God who delights in the torture of sinners."[22]

Roger Nicole objects to the first point, that God gives many people no chance to be saved. In Nicole's view, all that is required for an offer or invitation to be well-meant is the granting of the promised benefit upon satisfaction of whatever conditions are attached to the gift. According to Nicole, many exclusivists posit "a universal divine intention to save *on the condition* of repentance and faith. That is to say, *if only* human beings would repent and believe, they will be saved."[23]

---

21. I will say more about the inordinate role that emotionalism plays in pluralism and inclusivism in the next chapter. What is often made to look like an argument is nothing of the sort. It is simply an appeal to feeling, sentiment, or emotion.

22. Sanders, *No Other Name,* 114. The language in the cited allegations appear in Sanders's book. Sanders himself does not hold such beliefs.

23. Roger Nicole, "Universalism: Will Everyone Be Saved?" *Christianity Today* (20 March 1987): 32.

Of course, many exclusivists reject a literal understanding of hell. For example, J. P. Moreland and Gary Habermas write:

> We do not accept the idea that hell is a place where God actively tortures people forever and ever. There will indeed be everlasting, conscious, mental and physical torment in various degrees according to the lives people have lived here on earth. But the essence of that torment is relational in nature: the banishment from heaven and all it stands for. Mental and physical anguish result from the sorrow and shame of the judgment of being forever relationally excluded from God, heaven, and so forth. It is not due to God himself inflicting torture.[24]

According to William Crockett, even John Calvin and Martin Luther rejected strictly literal accounts of hell.[25] As Crockett understands the doctrine, "On the Judgment Day the wicked are separated from the righteous like chaff from grain, and they are carried far from the beauty and glory of God into a land of shadows where they contemplate what might have been. They are in the true sense of the word, lost forever."[26] Crockett identifies a number of contemporary evangelicals as holding similar views on the subject.[27]

It is clear that every member of our fallen and rebellious species deserves God's judgment. The various accounts of this judgment in Scripture help us understand how serious this entire matter is. Inclusivists know all too well how many conscientious exclusivists have wrestled with the details of this judgment, and it is shameful that some paint all exclusivists with the same brush of extreme literalism. Such tactics could be construed as a smokescreen for a weak defense of their position.[28]

---

24. Gary Habermas and J. P. Moreland, *Immortality: The Other Side of Death* (Nashville: Nelson, 1992), 169 – 70.

25. William Crockett, "The Metaphorical View," in *Four Views of Hell,* ed. William Crockett (Grand Rapids: Zondervan, 1992), 44.

26. Ibid., 62. Crockett is building on C. S. Lewis's view found in *The Problem of Pain* (New York: Macmillan, 1962), 126 – 27.

27. Crockett, *Four Views of Hell,* 44 – 45.

28. To his credit, John Sanders does not employ this tactic.

## CONCLUSION

The issues examined in this chapter raise even more doubts about inclusivism. The inclusivists' attack on exclusivism is more strident and the support for their views is much weaker than many realize upon their first encounter with these issues. Especially deplorable is the way inclusivists distort exclusivist thinking about important topics such as the doctrine of divine judgment. The more carefully inclusivism is studied, the weaker it looks.

Chapter Eleven

# WHY I AM NOT AN INCLUSIVIST

Inclusivism can have a strong emotional appeal for many evangelical Christians. Many could sleep better if there were less urgency or no urgency in getting the gospel to the unevangelized. Many of us have loved ones who died with their relationship to Christ uncertain or whose prospects for eternity appear bleak. Some comfort, however false it might prove to be, could be derived from various inclusivist theories noted in this book.

However, wise Christians know better than to confuse the truth with the way we would sometimes like things to be. Whatever the appeal to the heart, we must evaluate inclusivism with our minds. How inclusivism squares with Scripture is more important than how it makes us feel.

It is obvious from the discussion in this book that I am not an inclusivist. I have argued that inclusivism is seriously flawed in its theology. The way that inclusivists handle Scripture is disturbing in many respects. I have raised the question whether some inclusivists, such as Clark Pinnock, are not really exclusivists who believe in the possibility of salvation after death.

To conclude this discussion and this book, I want to deal with a few remaining issues that constitute additional reasons to question or reject inclusivism.

## THE INCLUSIVIST AS ROMANTIC

We sometimes refer to people as romantics when they give priority to feeling and emotion. Lutheran theologian Marc Mueller has described Pinnock's inclusivism as a "romantic project" that fails to reflect "a truly biblical understanding of the awesomeness of God's sovereignty over history, the nations and the world of men."[1] J. I. Packer believes inclusivists are more influenced by the "American idea of fairness" than by anything they have learned from Scripture.[2]

According to some, what we find in inclusivism is a troubling example of how good and sincere people allow their feelings to get the better of them. Once they convince themselves emotionally that a certain belief *must* be true, they conclude that it *is* true and must therefore be in the Bible. It is a matter of doing theology by imagination. Step after step, inclusivists indulge in heavy speculation. One speculation is laid on another until we have what is supposed to be an elaborate theological structure. Upon careful analysis, however, the system turns out to be a house of cards.

I have sought to say nothing in this book that implies that exclusivists lack concern for all the unevangelized who have died without Christ or for all the others for whom this fate is still future. When asked if there will be people in heaven who never had a chance to hear the gospel during their lifetime, the first thing a wise exclusivist will say is that he does not know. As Deuteronomy 29:29 states, "The secret things belong to the LORD our God, but the things revealed belong to us and to our children forever." Although we know about the Lamb's Book of Life (Rev. 20:12 – 15), we do not know whose names appear in it. But much that we do know suggests that men and women who have not confessed Christ as Savior will not be there.

There is much wisdom in Packer's advice that "[I]f we are wise, we shall not spend much time mulling over this notion [of the specific fate of specific unevangelized people]. Our job, after all, is to spread the gospel, not to guess what might happen to those to whom it never comes. Dealing with them is God's

---

1. Mueller's words appear in an unpublished response to Pinnock that was given during the 1989 annual meeting of the Evangelical Theological Society.

2. Packer's words are quoted by John Sanders from public comments made by Packer at a Trinity Evangelical Divinity School conference. See John Sanders, *No Other Name* (Grand Rapids: Eerdmans, 1992), 136. Readers familiar with the context surrounding the Packer quote will recognize, as I do, that there is more punch to Packer's words than Sanders recognizes.

business."[3] Genesis 18:25 asks, "Will not the Judge of all the earth do right?" Not only is it God's business, but also we can be certain that when God is finished dealing with all of us, none will be able to complain that they were treated unfairly.

John Sanders is sharply critical of thinking like this, labeling it "reverent agnosticism."[4] But as I have sought to demonstrate, I believe that Sanders fails to present good enough information or to make a strong enough case to justify his certainty on the question.

Roger Nicole has responded to Pinnock's supposition that heaven might contain some surprises for all of us. "My surprise," Nicole says, "might be to find in heaven more people than I expected; I shall be most happy about that. [Pinnock's] surprise may be to find substantially less. On balance, I prefer my potential surprise to his!"[5]

Nicole's words provide a natural transition to the quite different inclusivist and exclusivist attitudes toward evangelism and Christian missions.

## THE PESKY PROBLEM OF CHRISTIAN MISSIONS

Where inclusivism is concerned, the problem of Christian missions simply will not go away. Inclusivists like Pinnock and Sanders keep returning to the topic and are probably wise to do so. Even pluralist John Hick acknowledges that the major attraction of inclusivism "is that it negates the old missionary compulsion and yet is still Christocentric and still leaves Christianity in a uniquely central and normative position."[6]

Does inclusivism weaken missionary and evangelistic resolve? After admitting the appearance of a problem here, Pinnock usually begins with an ad hominem attack on exclusivists. Exclusivism does not always produce missionary zeal, he

---

3. J. I. Packer, *Christianity Today* (17 January 1986): 25.

4. Sanders, *No Other Name*, 17.

5. Roger Nicole, unpublished paper delivered at the 1989 annual meeting of the Evangelical Theological Society.

6. John Hick, *Disputed Questions in Theology and the Philosophy of Religion* (New Haven: Yale University Press, 1993), 143.

points out. He may feel that too many Christians who recognize the heathen as lost have chosen to do nothing about it. I would like nothing better than for this book to stir readers to a renewed concern for the lost.

By contrast, I do not see that inclusivism encourages people toward missions. In 1991 a polling organization surveyed people who work for Christian relief and development organizations with a view to gauging their level of concern toward missions and evangelism (the issue of attitude) and how much evangelism actually accompanies their important humanitarian work (the issue of practice). The poll also surveyed a large sampling of Christian laypeople who contribute to these relief and development organizations. Polling the laypeople served two purposes: (1) to show how much importance these donors attach to the relief and development groups' evangelism and missionary activity, and (2) to gauge how informed these donors are about the real priorities of the people running the organizations.[7]

The large majority of Christians who contribute to relief and development organizations not only want these groups to include evangelism as a top priority, but believe that these groups really do include more typical missionary activity among their primary tasks. Their contributions reflect their dual concern to help people with their material *and* spiritual needs. But the survey of relief and development staff revealed a quite different picture. Thirty-seven percent of the agency staff people did not endorse the statement that "the ultimate goal of economic development projects should be to spread the gospel and convert people to Christian faith."[8] Many people who work for relief and development organizations see their role as primarily or even exclusively one of providing humanitarian aid; evangelism and typical missionary activity are not seen as part of their task.

Does the survey reveal why so many people working in these organizations are indifferent to evangelism and missions activity? It is instructive in this connection to heed the conclu-

---

7. The significance of the poll is summarized by Amy Sherman in her article, "Where You Lead I will Follow?" *First Things* (February 1993): 5 – 6.

8. See Thomas Guterbock, "What Do Christians Expect From Christian Relief and Development?" *Stewardship Journal* 2 (Summer/Fall 1992):24.

sions of Thomas Guterbock, a secular social scientist, who examined the data.

> On the average, the agency staff [of relief and development organizations] are significantly lower than the Evangelical public in their commitment to the distinctiveness of Christian relief and development efforts. On several key issues, agency staff are substantially less likely to respond in ways that emphasize Christian distinctiveness. . . . The key predictor of which members of the agency staff express strong commitment to Christian distinctiveness is their personal theology. Particularly important is whether or not the staff member believes that personal Christian faith is the *only* route to salvation for people in other cultures — a point of doctrine that theologians call "exclusivity."

Guterbock concludes his analysis by stating that we

> may infer that there are strong pressures upon these [relief and development] professionals that tend in the direction of de-emphasizing the Christian aspect of their work. It seems that, once cast loose from their theological moorings, agency staff people are far more likely than members of the Evangelical public to modify their views on relief and development in a secular direction. If there may be other ways to heaven for the people of the Third World, then the imperative to evangelize is weakened as a logical result. If agency staff people face other circumstances or influences that work against that imperative, then this single change in theology opens the way for a major shift in policy and practice. . . . Our Survey of Christian Relief and Development Agencies has told us clearly that the specific theological beliefs of agency leaders and senior staff people are critical to understanding why a significant segment among them are less committed than members of the Evangelical public to the distinctiveness of Christian relief and development.[9]

Guterbock, it should be remembered, is a secular social scientist, but even he sees how a rejection of exclusivism weakens

---

9. The entire summer/fall issue of *Stewardship Journal* (1992) is devoted to analyses and evaluations of this important poll. The two long quotes from Guterbock appear in a separate survey booklet that is not yet published.

the resolve to place a high priority on evangelism when doing relief work.

Inclusivists like Pinnock and Sanders dismiss such comments. Sanders argues that "Just because some people feel it a crucial motivating factor to believe all the unevangelized are lost does not make it true that they are lost. Besides, there may be good reasons to continue missionary activity even if there is hope for the evangelized without it."[10] Sanders offers an interesting example to support his point.

> It is important to note that an argument from utility does not necessarily establish truth. In order to get my children to hurry up and get ready for church, I might tell them that it is 9:15 when it is actually only 9:00. If the strategy works, I don't take that as evidence that it really is 9:00. Similarly, even if it is true that a belief in [exclusivism] leads to stronger support from [sic] missions, this does not tell us anything about the truth of [exclusivist] beliefs. And, conversely, if belief in the wider hope were conclusively shown to reduce support for missions, this would not in itself indicate that the wider hope view was false; the problem might well lie elsewhere — in an inadequate theory of missions, for instance.[11]

Let us agree that the utility of a theory or practice does not establish its truth. Of course, a sword this sharp cuts both ways. It also rules out any attempts to sway people by appealing to their emotions. Just because inclusivism makes people feel better doesn't make *it* true.

But I believe Sanders misconstrues the exclusivists' concerns about missions. At no point in this book have I suggested that inclusivism's negative effect upon certain forms of Christian activity proves the falsity of inclusivism. So what are we to make of the survey of people involved in certain relief and development organizations? Throughout this book I have been arguing that ideas have consequences. In most of it I have tried to show the theoretical or theological consequences of inclusivist ideas. But it is also important to show that inclusivist ideas have

10. John Sanders, "Is Belief in Christ Necessary for Salvation?" *Evangelical Quarterly* 60 (1988): 248.
11. Sanders, *No Other Name*, 283 – 84.

practical consequences as well. These consequences do not prove inclusivism false, but they do matter.

John Sanders concludes his book *No Other Name* with a very strong philosophy of Christian missions.[12] It is good enough that directors of Christian relief and development organizations ought to consider requiring their employees to read it. But as we have now seen so often, what inclusivists give with their right hands they often take back with their left. His impressive philosophy of missions notwithstanding, Sanders not only denies the necessity of evangelizing those who have not heard the gospel, but also holds out the possibility that many who have actually rejected the gospel after hearing it may still end up being saved. In Sanders's words, "[R]efusal to accept the church's invitation should not be equated with refusal to accept God's invitation."[13]

I close this section with the following comments. I agree with Sanders that whatever effect inclusivism might have upon evangelism and missions fails to prove that inclusivism is false. However, other sections of part 2 of this book provide ample reasons to think inclusivism is false. It is one thing for a theory to be false; harmless errors can sometimes be ignored. But errors that strongly dispose people toward actions that can compromise the church's mission on earth and place obstacles in the way of evangelism are much too serious to overlook.

## DO INCLUSIVISTS TEACH SALVATION BY HUMAN WORKS?

Once again we confront an issue on which it appears that inclusivists want to walk down both sides of the street at the same time. On the one hand, John Sanders takes the historic evangelical position that no humans "are saved by their own moral efforts."[14] On the other hand, he ignores inclusivist implications to the exact opposite. Sanders affirms Pinnock's understanding of the parable of the sheep and the goats in Matthew 25:31 – 40 as an indication that serving the poor is an adequate

---

12. See ibid., 284 – 85.
13. Ibid., 237.
14. Ibid., 235.

substitute for faith and may count as one ground on which God saves the unevangelized.[15]

Pinnock has written, "Surely God judges the heathen in relation to the light they have, not according to the light that did not reach them. Of course God condemns those who really are his enemies. But his judgment will take into account what people are conscious of, what they yearn for, what they have suffered, what they do out of love, and so forth."[16] In *A Wideness in God's Mercy*, Pinnock talks about God's *ethical criterion* for salvation and then asks, "What if only the ethical criterion is apparent in a person? What if the person seems genuine according to the ethical criterion, but not a believer according to the cognitive one?"[17]

In other words, Pinnock is suggesting that a person who lacks New Testament faith but produces good works of a certain kind may still be saved on that basis. Pinnock goes so far as to speculate about God's saving "even the atheist who, though rejecting God (as he understands God), responds positively to him implicitly by acts of love shown to the neighbor."[18] The reader should reflect on these words and the meaning they give to salvation. The reader should also meditate upon the negative effect these convictions are bound to have on the future shape of Christian thought and action.

In an earlier chapter we noticed a few evangelicals who have expressed concern over what they saw as a drift toward Pelagianism in some inclusivists. But that warning was uttered largely in connection with the tendency of some Arminians to view saving faith as a human work contributing to salvation. Now we find Pinnock suggesting that not even faith is necessary and that perhaps certain kinds of decent human conduct will serve just as well. I believe that all this is serious enough that Pinnock will reconsider his remarks and retract statements like these.

---

15. See ibid., 259.
16. Clark Pinnock, "Toward an Evangelical Theology of Religions," *Journal of the Evangelical Theological Society* 33 (1990): 367 – 68.
17. Clark Pinnock, *A Wideness in God's Mercy* (Grand Rapids: Zondervan, 1992), 98.
18. Ibid.

## PLURALISM AND INCLUSIVISM ON SCRIPTURE:
## A DISTURBING SIMILARITY

Douglas Geivett recently drew attention to a troublesome parallel between the pilgrimage of John Hick and that being taken by Clark Pinnock and other inclusivists. Geivett notes that Hick's "transformation took place somewhat gradually, as important philosophical commitments controlled the outworking of his theological views. A propositional view of divine revelation was an early casualty for Hick. Intuitions about what a loving God could be up to in allowing evil pushed him in the direction of universalism. Having forsaken the divine authority of the Bible, no amount of careful exegesis could cure him of his universalist impulse."[19]

It is helpful that Geivett focuses on Hick's early abandonment of the evangelical view of Scripture, which saw him first reject any suggestion that divine special revelation might contain vital information or truth.[20] While Hick stayed rather close to orthodoxy during the years he flirted with a neo-liberal view of Scripture, once the authority of the Bible was no longer a controlling factor in his theology there was nothing left within historic Christianity to prevent the far more radical musings of his later years. His footsteps down the path to pluralism are recognizable by the discarded beliefs one finds along the way. Hick came to reject the Incarnation, the Trinity, the deity of Christ, the Resurrection, the Atonement, and every other essential Christian belief. And although Hick continues to identify himself as a Christian, no essential Christian belief remains in his thinking.

Geivett is struck by certain alarming similarities between John Hick at the early stages of his career and the attempt of Clark Pinnock to provide for the salvation of non-Christians and even some anti-Christians in a way that stops short of pluralism.

---

19. The quotations from Douglas Geivett in this chapter come from a personal letter to the author dated December 3, 1992. His words are used with his permission.

20. For a longer discussion of similar moves by other liberal theologians in the twentieth century, see Ronald Nash, *The Word of God and the Mind of Man* (Phillipsburg, N.J.: Presbyterian and Reformed, 1992).

Some inclusivists' views of the "wideness of God's mercy," Geivett warns, appear

> to be motivated by a similar sentimentalism about the love of God. It is their conviction that the Bible speaks with divine authority that seems to be keeping them (for now) from taking the ominous final step. But the exegetical support for their view is so fragile that one can only wonder how they can resist the temptation to go the way of John Hick. Capitulation must come pretty easily when sentiment is a fundamental control on one's hermeneutics.[21]

One hopes that Geivett will be proved wrong, but one fears that should some inclusivists ever find reason to reject inclusivism, they would choose pluralism over exclusivism.

## INCLUSIVISM AND THE BOOK OF ACTS

I begin this section with a suggestion or challenge, as the case may be: Begin with the assumption that inclusivism is true and then read the entire book of Acts through inclusivist lenses. As you examine the messages delivered by Peter, Philip, Paul, and others in Acts, try to place yourself in their sandals and ask whether an inclusivist would have said and done the things that are recorded. I proceeded to read through Acts in this way and was stunned by what I discovered.

For example, if I had been an inclusivist present on the Day of Pentecost, I would have been struck by Peter's emphasis on sin and the remission of sins that is available in Jesus Christ. I find Pinnock and Sanders strangely silent on the matter of the sin problem of unevangelized believers. Had I been an inclusivist, I would not have uttered Peter's words in Acts 2:38: "Repent and be baptized every one of you, in the name of Jesus Christ for the forgiveness of your sins." Peter's point here is clearly anti-inclusivist, strongly implying that if his hearers did not get their relationship with Jesus Christ right, their sins would not be forgiven.

---

21. For samples of this troubling insinuation, see Clark Pinnock, "Toward an Evangelical Theology of Missions," 362, and John Sanders, *No Other Name*, 106.

Had I been Peter in that setting and also an inclusivist, I would have said something like this: "Now friends, I don't want any of you thinking that I'm intolerant or narrow-minded in any way. I know that many of you are already saved because you've been faithfully seeking God as best you can. I want those of you in my audience who fit that description to know that I'm not preaching at you. It's the rest of you — you sinners — who must repent and be baptized if your sins are to be forgiven. For those of you who are already saved, I'm offering you an opportunity for something more fulfilling." No, I'm afraid that had I been the speaker that day and also been an inclusivist, I would not have been as specific and restrictive as Peter.

Had I been in Paul's sandals, I would have answered the famous question of the Philippian jailer in a rather different way. When he asked, "Men, what must I do to be saved?" (Acts 16:30), a good inclusivist would have advised him to calm down and realize that he may already be saved. Perhaps we could dialogue for a while and examine his relationship to the saving content of general revelation. Perhaps we would discover that he was already one of several million non-Christian believers in the world. Would not an inclusivist avoid saying Paul's severely restricting phrase, "Believe in the Lord Jesus, and you will be saved" (Acts 16:31)?

Even the most cursory reading of Acts will reveal the way in which almost every message in the book emphasizes the death and resurrection of Christ. Inclusivists, as we have seen, insist that the gospel does not have these two events as its central focus. They claim that Paul spoke of the gospel in these terms only because that was an appropriate message for the people of Corinth to hear. The implication is that some other gospel that makes no reference to the death and resurrection of Jesus would serve in another place at another time.

But why, then, did all those early gospel messages always emphasize the same thing, namely, that Christ died for our sins and rose again? I submit that if Paul had been an inclusivist, he would never have uttered the following words to an audience of Jews who had just rejected the gospel: "We had to speak the word of God to you first. Since you reject it *and do not consider yourselves worthy of eternal life,* we now turn to the Gentiles" (Acts 13:46, italics mine). In these words Paul indicates not that his audience's loss of eternal life became effective at that moment, but that they were devoid of it prior to hearing the gospel. As far as he could tell, their names were not written in the Book of Life (see Rev. 17:8).

How could an inclusivist have said what Paul states in Acts 20:26 – 27: "Therefore, I declare to you today that I am innocent of the blood of all men. For I have not hesitated to proclaim to you the whole will of God." If Paul had not been faithful in proclaiming the gospel, he would have had blood on his hands. This is no way for an inclusivist to think. Even if Christians fail to carry the gospel to the unevangelized, there is little or no culpability regarding "the blood of men" because God is saving unevangelized people all the time.

And finally, had I been Paul and an inclusivist, I would have been totally shocked by what God said when he called me: "I am sending you to open their eyes and turn them from darkness to light, and from the power of Satan to God, so that they may receive forgiveness of sins and a place among those who are sanctified by faith in me" (Acts 26:18). This survey through the book of Acts makes it clear that Peter and Paul did not speak and act like inclusivists. Acts 26:18 helps us see that *God* does not speak or act like an inclusivist either.

## CONCLUSION

I close this book by inviting the reader to reflect on the spiritual condition of Saul of Tarsus before his conversion. Saul had passed every test of inclusivist salvation. He satisfied Clark Pinnock's Faith Principle, drawn from Hebrews 11:6, with plenty to spare: Saul not only believed that God exists, but was diligently seeking him. But there is even more to say about Saul's religious zeal: He was a Jew who sought Yahweh with such diligence that he participated in the persecution and murder of Yahweh's enemies (Acts 22:20).

It is appropriate here to reread Paul's own description of his pre-conversion zeal for God in Acts 26:4 – 5 and Philippians

3:4 – 6. If inclusivism is true, then Saul the Pharisee was saved. But, we note, this judgment was not shared by Paul the apostle (Phil. 3:7 – 11). Even though Saul satisfied every requirement of the inclusivists' Faith Principle, Saul was still a lost sinner (1 Tim. 1:15).

We all know that if we begin with a premise that says *If A, then B* and then discover that *B* is false, we must conclude that *A* is false. Applying this logic to our present case, we quickly see that the following argument is sound: If inclusivism is true, then Saul of Tarsus was saved. But it is false that Saul was saved. Therefore, inclusivism is not true.

As we have seen, inclusivism has become an enormously influential position among evangelicals at the end of the twentieth century. Given the weaknesses of inclusivism that we have noted, it seems obvious that inclusivist evangelicals need to think further on these matters. For many of them, I suspect that inclusivism has appeared to be a relatively painless way to resolve difficulties about the fate of the unevangelized; it certainly makes a powerful appeal to our emotions. But I have tried to show that the adoption of inclusivism is not theologically harmless. The acceptance of this biblically unsupportable opinion carries an enormously high theological cost. One hopes that large numbers of evangelicals already committed to inclusivism will see these dangers and recognize the weaknesses of the position they have accepted in such a careless and unthinking way.

# SELECTED BIBLIOGRAPHY

Aldwickle, Russell F. *Jesus — A Savior or the Savior?* Macon, Ga.: Mercer University Press, 1982.

Almond, P. "John Hick's Copernican Revolution." *Theology* 86 (1983). 36 – 41.

Anderson, Gerald, and Thomas F. Stransky, eds. *Christ's Lordship and Religious Pluralism.* Maryknoll, N.Y.: Orbis Books, 1981.

_____. *Mission Trends Number 5: Faith Meets Faith.* Grand Rapids: Eerdmans, 1981.

Anderson, Sir Norman. *Christianity and Comparative Religion.* 2d ed. Leicester, Eng.: Inter-Varsity Press, 1984.

Barnes, Michael. *Christian Identity and Religious Pluralism.* Nashville: Abingdon, 1989.

Basinger, David. "Hick's Religious Pluralism and 'Reformed Epistemology': A Middle Ground." *Faith and Philosophy* 5 (1988). 421 – 32.

Blue, J. Ronald. "Untold Billions: Are They Really Lost?" *Bibliotheca Sacra* 138 (1981). 338 – 50.

Byrne, P. "John Hick's Philosophy of Religion." *Scottish Journal of Theology* 35 (1982). 289 – 301.

Carruthers, Gregory H., S.J. *The Uniqueness of Jesus Christ in the Theocentric Model of the Christian Theology of World Religions.* Lanham, Md.: University Press of America, 1990.

Christian, W. *Oppositions of Religious Doctrines.* London: Macmillan, 1972.

Cobb, John B., Jr. *Christ in a Pluralistic Age.* Philadelphia: Westminster, 1975.

_____. "The Meaning of Pluralism for Christian Self-Understanding." In *Religious Pluralism,* ed. Leroy S. Rouner, 161 – 79. South Bend, Ind.: University of Notre Dame Press, 1984.

Coward, H. *Pluralism: Challenge to World Religions.* Maryknoll, N.Y.: Orbis Books, 1985.

Crockett, William V., and James G. Sigountos, eds. *Through No Fault of Their Own?* Grand Rapids: Baker, 1991.

Danielou, Jean. *Holy Pagans of the Old Testament.* Translated by Felix Faber. London: Longmans, Green, 1957.

Davis, Charles. *Christ and the World Religions.* London: Hodder & Stoughton, 1970.

Dawe, Donald G., and John B. Carman, eds. *Christian Faith in a Religiously Plural World.* Maryknoll, N.Y.: Orbis Books, 1981.

D'Costa, Gavin. "Taking Other Religions Seriously: Some Ironies in the Current Debate on a Christian Theology of Religions." *The Thomist* 54 (1990). 519 – 29.

D'Costa, Gavin, ed. *Christian Uniqueness Reconsidered.* Maryknoll, N.Y.: Orbis Books, 1990.

____. *John Hick's Theology of Religions.* Lanham, Md.: University Press of America, 1987.

____. "The Pluralist Paradigm in the Christian Theology of Religions." *Scottish Journal of Theology* 39 (1986). 211 – 24.

____. *Theology and Religious Pluralism.* New York: Basil Blackwell, 1986.

____. "Karl Rahner's Anonymous Christian: A Reappraisal." *Modern Theology* 1 (1985). 131 – 48.

Drummond, R. H. *Gautama the Buddha: An Essay in Religious Understanding.* Grand Rapids: Eerdmans, 1974.

Dunn, James D. G. *Christology in the Making.* Philadelphia: Westminster, 1980.

Forrester, D. "Professor Hick and the Universe of Faiths." *Scottish Journal of Theology* 29 (1976). 65 – 72.

Geivett, R. Douglas. *Evil and the Evidence for God: The Challenge of John Hick's Theodicy.* Philadelphia: Temple University Press, 1994.

Glasser, A. F. "A Paradigm Shift?" *Missiology* 9 (1981). 393 – 408.

Goulder, Michael, ed. *Incarnation and Myth: The Debate Continued.* London: SCM Press, 1979.

Green, Michael, ed. *The Truth of God Incarnate.* London: Hodder & Stoughton, 1977.

Griffiths, Paul, and Delmas Lewis. "On Grading Religions, Seeking Truth, and Being Nice to People — A Reply to Professor Hick." *Religious Studies* 19 (1983). 75 – 80.

Griffiths, Paul, ed. *Christianity Through Non-Christian Eyes.* Maryknoll, N.Y.: Orbis Books, 1990.

Gundry, Robert H. "Salvation According to Scripture: No Middle Ground." *Christianity Today* 22 (1977). 342 – 44.

Hebblethwaite, B. "The Status of Anonymous Christians." *Heythrop Journal* (1977). 47 – 55.

Hebblethwaite, B., and John Hick. *Christianity and Other Religions.* London: Collins, 1980.

Hengel, Martin. *The Son of God.* Philadelphia: Fortress, 1976.

Hewitt, Harold, ed. *Problems in the Philosophy of Religion: Critical Studies* of the Work of John Hick. New York: St. Martin's Press, 1991.

Hick, John. Disputed Questions in Theology and the Philosophy of Religion. New Haven: Yale University Press, 1993.

_____. An Interpretation of Religion. New Haven: Yale University Press, 1989.

_____. "An Inspiration Christology for a Religiously Plural World." In Encountering Jesus, ed. Stephen Davis. Philadelphia: Fortress, 1988.

_____. "The Non-Absoluteness of Christianity." In The Myth of Christian Uniqueness, ed. John Hick and Paul Knitter. Maryknoll, N.Y.: Orbis Books, 1987.

_____. Problems of Religious Pluralism. New York: St Martin's Press, 1985.

_____. "A Philosophy of Religious Pluralism." In The World's Religious Traditions: Current Perspectives in Religious Studies. Essays in Honour of Wilfred Cantwell Smith, ed. F. Whaling. 147 – 64. Edinburgh: T. & T. Clark, 1984.

_____. "The Theology of Pluralism." Theology 86 (1983). 335 – 40.

_____. "On Grading Religions." Religious Studies 17 (1981). 451 – 67.

_____. "Pluralism and the Reality of the Transcendent." In Theologians in Transition, ed. James M. Wall. New York: Crossroad, 1981.

_____. God Has Many Names. London: Macmillan, 1980.

_____. The Centre of Christianity. London: SCM Press, 1977.

_____. God and the Universe of Faiths. London: Macmillan, 1973.

Hick, John, ed. The Myth of God Incarnate. London: SCM Press, 1977.

_____. Truth and Dialogue in World Religions. Philadelphia: Westminster Press, 1974.

Jathanna, Origen. The Decisiveness of the Christ Event and the Universality of Christianity in a World of Religious Plurality. Berne, Switz.: P. Lang, 1981.

Jeremias, Joachim. New Testament Theology: The Proclamation of Jesus. New York: Scribner's, 1971.

Knitter, Paul. No Other Name? A Critical Survey of Christian Attitudes Toward The World Religions. Maryknoll, N.Y.: Orbis Books, 1985.

Kraemer, Hendrik. Religion and the Christian Faith. London: Lutterworth Press, 1956.

_____. The Christian Message in a Non-Christian World. Grand Rapids: Kregel, 1938.

Kung, Hans, and Juergen Moltmann, eds. Christianity Among World Religions. Edinburgh: T. & T. Clark, 1986.

Lindsell, Harold. An Evangelical Theology of Missions. Grand Rapids: Zondervan, 1970.

Mathis, T. Against John Hick. Lanham, Md.: University Press of America, 1985.

Moule, C. *The Origin of Christology*. New York: Cambridge University Press, 1977.

Nash, Ronald H. *Great Divides*. Colorado Springs: NavPress, 1993.

____. *The Gospel and the Greeks*. Dallas: Probe Books, 1992.

____. *The Word of God and the Mind of Man*. Phillipsburg, N.J.: Presbyterian and Reformed, 1992.

____. *Worldviews in Conflict*. Grand Rapids: Zondervan, 1992.

____. *Faith and Reason*. Grand Rapids: Zondervan, 1988.

Nash, Ronald H., ed. *Process Theology*. Grand Rapids: Baker, 1987.

____. *Christian Faith and Historical Understanding*. Dallas: Probe Books, 1983.

____. *The Concept of God*. Grand Rapids: Zondervan, 1983.

Nash, Ronald, and Humberto Belli. *Beyond Liberation Theology*. Grand Rapids: Baker, 1992.

Neill, Stephen. *Christian Faith and Other Faiths*. New York: Oxford University Press, 1970.

Netland, Harold. *Dissonant Voices*. Grand Rapids: Eerdmans, 1991.

____. "Exclusivism, Tolerance and Truth." *Missiology* 15 (1987). 77 – 95.

Neuner, Joseph, ed. *Christian Revelation and World Religions*. London: Burns & Oates, 1967.

Newbigin, Lesslie. *Christian Witness in a Plural Society*. London: British Council of Churches, 1977.

____. *The Finality of Christ*. London: SCM Press, 1969.

Panikkar, Raimundo. *The Unknown Christ of Hinduism*. London: Darton Longman and Todd, 1964.

Pinnock, Clark. *A Wideness in God's Mercy*. Grand Rapids: Zondervan, 1992.

____. "Acts 4:12 — No Other Name Under Heaven." In *Through No Fault of Their Own?* ed. William V. Crockett and James G. Sigountos. Grand Rapids: Baker, 1991.

____. "Toward an Evangelical Theology of Religions." *Journal of the Evangelical Theological Society* 33 (1990). 359 – 68.

____. "The Finality of Jesus Christ in a World of Religions." In *Christian Faith and Practice in the Modern World*, ed. Mark A. Noll and David F. Wells. Grand Rapids: Eerdmans, 1988. 152 – 68.

____. "Why Is Jesus the Only Way?" *Eternity* 27 (1976). 13 – 34.

Race, Alan. *Christians and Religious Pluralism*. Maryknoll, N.Y.: Orbis Books, 1983.

Rahner, Karl. *Revelation and Tradition*. New York: Herder & Herder, 1966.

____. *Theological Investigations*. 20 vols. New York: Seabury, 1966 – 83.

Robinson, John A.T. *Truth Is Two-Eyed*. London: SCM Press, 1979.

Sanders, John. *No Other Name*. Grand Rapids: Eerdmans, 1992.

_____. "Is Belief in Christ Necessary for Salvation?" *Evangelical Quarterly* (1988). 241 – 59.

Samartha, S. *The Hindu Response to the Unbound Christ*. Madras: Christian Literature Society, 1974.

Smart, Ninian. *The Religious Experience of Mankind*. New York: Scribner's, 1969.

_____. *World Religions: A Dialogue*. London: Pelican, 1960.

Smith, Wilfred Cantwell. *Towards a World Theology*. Philadelphia: Westminster Press, 1981.

_____. *Faith and Belief*. Princeton, N.J.: Princeton University Press, 1979.

_____. *Questions of Religious Truth*. New York: Scribner's, 1967.

_____. *The Faith of Other Men*. New York: New American Library, 1963.

_____. *The Meaning and End of Religion*. New York: Harper & Row, 1962.

Tillich, Paul. *Christianity and the Encounter of the World Religions*. New York: Columbia University Press, 1963.

Trigg, Roger. "Religion and the Threat of Relativism." Religious Studies 19 (1983). 297 – 310.

# INDEX OF PERSONS AND TOPICS

182

*Is Jesus the Only Savior?*

D'Costa, Gavin, 29, 103, 110
Demarest, Bruce 20, 21, 119, 120,
136, 159
*Dharma* 46
Dyrness, William 108

Eddy, Paul 10, 13, 14
Epicycles 31, 32
— in Hick's pluralism 32, 34, 35
— in Ptolemaic astronomy 31, 32
— in theology 32, 35, 111
Epistemology 24, 39, 40
Eschatological verification 98 – 99
Evangelism 10, 106, 126, 165 – 69
Excluded Middle, law of 54, 55, 56
Exclusivism Chap. Two *passim* 33,
34, 35, 37, 38, 92, 99
Experience, religious 67

Fackre, Gabriel 158
Faith
— Inclusivist view of 113, 123 –
26, 169 – 70
— W. C. Smith's view of 59 – 60
"Faith Principle" 124 – 26, 174
Feminist theology 10, 49 – 51
Form-criticism 77 – 80
Forrester, D. 37

Geivett, Douglas 10, 22, 37, 74, 81,
94, 99 – 100, 171, 172
Gentiles, salvation of 129, 140 – 41
Gentry, Kenneth, Jr. 10, 24
God 12, 20, 21, 34, 46, 119, 120,
125, 133, 134, 139
— attributes of 36, 37, 85, 97
— essential properties of 85
— Hick's unknown/unknowable
36, 37, 41 – 44, 64, 97
— knowledge about 33, 36
— and knowledge of future 130,
131, 132, 149

— loving 33, 35
— noumenal 40, 41, 43, 51
— omniscience of 85, 130, 131
— personal/impersonal 33, 36, 43
— personality of 33, 35, 36
— phenomenal 40, 41, 43, 51
— power of 85, 131
— properties of 33, 43, 44
— relation to good and evil 43
Gospel 126, 173
— inclusivist's version of 118 –
19, 132, 133
Great Commission 106, 138
Griffiths, Paul 93
Gruenler, Royce 74
Grudem, Wayne 158
Guterbock, Thomas 167

Habermas, Gary 161
Hackett, Stuart 108
Hell 19, 20, 96 – 97, 115, 160 – 61
Hengel, Martin 82
Hick, John 13, 18, 19, 22, 23, 25, 92,
93, 94, 95, 96, 97, 98, 103, 111,
165, 171, 172
— and the Bible 13, 14, 15
— and Christology Chap. Five
*passim*
— and development of early pluralism Chap. Two *passim*
— and development of later pluralism Chap. Three *passim*
— and Eastern religions 99, 100
— and feminism 49 – 51
— and God 33
— and historical skepticism 77 –
84
— and logic 53 – 55
— and myth 71 – 72, 75 – 76
— objections to Hick's early pluralism 34 – 48
— objections to Hick's later plu-

# INDEX OF SCRIPTURE REFERENCES